Poul Jorgensen's

MODERN
TROUT FLIES

and how to tie them

Poul Jorgensen's

MODERN
TROUT FLIES

and how to tie them

Color Photographs by Lee Boltin

with additional photographs by Poul Jorgensen

Black and white photographs by Poul Jorgensen

NICK LYONS BOOKS

DOUBLEDAY & COMPANY, INC., GARDEN CITY, NEW YORK   1979

I would like to thank all the fly tyers from around the world who send me flies. I am sorry we could not include them all. A special note of gratitude goes to two good friends and fine fly tyers, Ralph Graves and Phil Pirone, for assisting me in research for this project and for their invaluable suggestions and other help.

–P.J.

© 1975, 1979 by Poul Jorgensen and Lee Boltin

All Rights Reserved
Printed in the United States of America
ISBN: 0-385-15346-5
ISBN: 0-385-15347-3 pbk.
Library of Congress Catalog Card Number: 79-03897

Designed by Ruth Kolbert

FIRST EDITION

*Portions of this book originally appeared
in the Poul Jorgensen Trout Fly Charts
Published by Shadowbrook Publications*

NICK LYONS BOOKS
IS A DIVISION OF ERNEST BENN
NEW YORK AND LONDON

CONTENTS

FOREWORD

I STILL HAVE A VIVID MEMORY OF THE MANY SUMMERS I SPENT AS A youngster in my native country of Denmark. My father took me fishing regularly for pickerel and perch, which in their own special way were challenging for a youngster with a thirst for fishing adventure. We didn't do much trout fishing in those days, but the few times I did go, it was especially exciting. Sometimes my father got an invitation to fish some leased club water and took me along, or he would get permission to fish a stream that was situated on private land where only the owner and his close friends could fish.

Now things are changed! Today trout fishing is no longer reserved for the select few—it is available to anyone who cares to participate, and there is enough accessible fishing water to go around. This change in culture brought about an era of sophisticated fishing equipment, and with it, the sophisticated angler—one who not only fishes whenever he can, but one who is also a collector of rods, reels, and scores of other "nondescript curiosities" related to his angling sport. However, the most fascinating things about fly fishing—aside from the fishing itself—are the flies and how to tie them. As I am reflecting on the past, and we all do occasionally, I am delighted to say that I am one of the very fortunate fellows who has had the privilege of participating in that enjoyable aspect of the sport for more than twenty years.

During that period of time I have seen fly tying evolve from a relatively infant stage, by comparison, to one of the most important aspects of the sport of fly fishing.

Angling historians, I am sure, would probably ask you to leaf back in time to the fifteenth century and to Dame Juliana Berners, or perhaps to the Macedonians, for an answer to the beginning of artificial flies and fly dressing. This may well be appropriate for historians, but the modern angler and fly tyer has trouble enough keeping up with all the new developments, new flies, new materials, and new books that appear almost daily; he prefers to stay in the present and learn all he can. Besides, some of the old timers who developed many of the flies we use today are still around, both in the United States and other countries, and it is they who in my opinion should be applauded for sharing with us. In reality, this book is the result of their pioneering and teaching, combined with the outstanding efforts of contemporary tyers from around the world.

I do not intend this to be an "instructional" fly tying book covering all aspects of fly dressing from one end of the spectrum to the other, but rather to serve as a fly reference and identification code for both the fly tyers and also those fly fishermen who do not tie their own flies. For the fly fisherman, I am hopeful that the book will enable him to identify the flies he has purchased over the past seasons so he can compare them with the fine color photos and descriptions found on the pages that follow. In that way he can select his future purchases more intelligently. For the fly tyer, I hope Lee Boltin's and my photographs will show the colors, shapes, and styles of tying that the original patterns called for. For the less accomplished fly tyer, I have also included a section describing the most essential tools, hooks, and materials, in addition to some basic fly-tying instructions that, if closely followed, will enable even the novice to tie a fishing fly that he can be proud of.

The flies themselves are divided into four categories: nymphs, wet flies, dry flies, and streamers. In each of these categories the flies are arranged alphabetically, with a color photograph and an abbreviated list of materials needed to tie each fly. Since this somewhat skimpy description may not be sufficient information for some, you can get more detailed clarification by referring to the various other sections in the book dealing with tools and materials, including the all-important "Tying Tips," a section that gives special and specific advice on how to tie the flies shown in the color section.

Every fly in this book was carefully selected from among many patterns. It was often hard to leave out some of the "supercontraptions" recommended by well-meaning friends. I do believe, however, that the ones included will cover most of your needs for fishing anywhere in the world.

Fly tying is an art—a school from which we never graduate. I have always liked to experiment, and I guess it's kind of a trademark for fly tyers: if something works it must be changed. Therefore, I heartily encourage experimentation with patterns.

POUL JORGENSEN

1

TOOLS, HOOKS and MATERIALS

TOOLS

IT IS FORTUNATE THAT THERE ARE RELATIVELY FEW TOOLS REQUIRED for fly tying, so one can afford to acquire a complete set right at the outset. It is always best to get the finest available, and the better the tools the longer they last if properly cared for. The following is a list and description of the only tools you need for tying a good fly—in addition to a lot of practice.

The Vise

I don't know if I can emphasize strongly enough that it is important to get the very best vise you can afford. It is by far the most important tool you will be using. It must be made of the finest steel and designed to hold hooks from size 28 to 3/0. There are many models available today

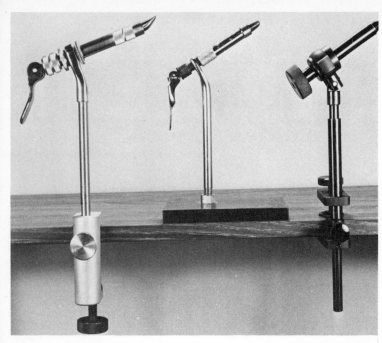

Three vises *(left to right):* the HMH Vise,
Thompson A Vise, and the Price Vise.

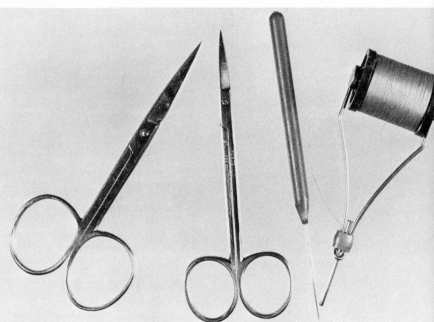

Left to right: heavy-duty scissors, Iris scissors, dubbing needle, and bobbin.

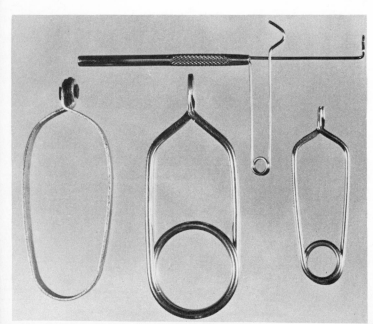

Top row: whip-finishing tool. *Below, left to right:* Thompson's
rubber-jaw hackle pliers, English-style heavy pliers,
and English-type midge pliers.

either on a stand or with a table clamp. Before you buy one, I suggest you see it and try it if at all possible. A vise is a very personal thing.

Scissors

It is practical to have two pairs of scissors. One pair should be of the fine-pointed variety; I can highly recommend the surgeon's Iris scissors, which are about four and a half inches long, for cutting hackles, thread, and other fine delicate material. The second pair should be of about the same length, but heavy-duty scissors with sturdier blades for trimming quills, tinsel, and the like. Good scissors always last longer than cheap ones, and next to the vise they are probably the most important tools.

Hackle Pliers

This tool is designed to hold the hackle while it is being wound; the inexpensive, rubber-jawed pliers manufactured by Thompson are about the best available. In addition, I use a second pair of the heavier English design. They are particularly handy when spinning dubbing in a loop, and whenever a pair of heavy sturdy pliers is needed. For very small flies you can add a third pair, which are also of English design.

Bobbin

Designed to hold the thread spool, the bobbin helps to prevent the thread from unraveling while it hangs by its weight as you prepare material. Before the bobbin existed, the tyer would make a half hitch whenever he stopped working on the fly.

Dubbing Needle

This is the most inexpensive tool you need, and it can be homemade. A small piece of dowel with a sewing needle inserted in the end will work very well. They are, however, available from your supplier in various designs, either with a metal or wooden handle. The tool is used for spreading fur on the tying thread, for applying cement on fly heads, and for similar chores.

Whip Finisher

This tool is for finishing off the tying thread after the fly is completed and the head has been wound. A demonstration of how to work the tool is illustrated in the chapter dealing with fly-tying basics.

Additional Tools

There are some nonessential tools available from the supplier that can be handy at times; these include the half-hitch tool, the stacker (for aligning hair), the hackle gauge, the electric fur blender, and several others. After you have been tying for a while you can make up your own mind as to what you need other than the essential fly-tying tools.

HOOKS

It is important to have a good selection of hooks to choose from so you can tie all the flies in different sizes for both surface and subsurface fishing. Most suppliers who deal exclusively in fly-tying supplies have a catalogue that explains the many hook types that are manufactured specifically for fishing flies.

Dry-Fly Hooks

These hooks are manufactured of light-wire stock specifically for dry flies. There are two types I use most frequently: the Mustad #94833 and #94842. The first model has a turned-down eye, the other a turned-up eye. Both types are made from extra-fine wire and have a round bend. The #94842 is particularly important when dressing the flies that float in their fur body where the eye may otherwise be in the surface film and give a distorted view of the fly from underwater. They are also used for spinner-type flies. Both hook models are available in sizes 8 through 28.

DRY FLY HOOKS
Mustad #94833

Mustad #94842

Wet-Fly and Nymph Hooks

This type of hook is made with heavy wire to make them sink better. I prefer the Sproat Bend Mustad #3906 and #3906B. The difference between the two is found in the length. The #3906B is a little longer in the shank than the other. They are available in sizes 4 through 20.

WET-FLY AND NYMPH HOOKS
Mustad #3906

Mustad #37160
English bait hook

Streamer Hooks

The two types of hooks I prefer for streamers and bucktails are different both in length and hook bend. Mustad #3665A is 6X long and has a limerick bend, whereas the Mustad #79580 is 4X long and has a round bend. Both hooks are excellent for tying most of the streamers in this book. They are available in sizes 2 through 16.

STREAMER HOOKS
Mustad #3665A
6X long

Mustad #79580
4X long

Other Hooks

The hooks I have described are those I prefer to use, but that doesn't mean that they are the only ones available. If you look through a supplier's catalog you may very well find some that you like better than those suggested.

MATERIAL

The material list for a fly tyer is never-ending, and new items are being added every day. One can surely say that a good collection takes a lifetime to accumulate. To tie some flies just to fish with, however, it is not necessary to have feathers and fur from every bird and animal in existence. It is far better to pay attention to just those items that are essential and acquire the rest a few at a time. The following description of materials is by no means complete, but merely a start; they will enable you to dress all the most important flies.

Sundry Items

Head Cement

A good clear lacquer is needed, primarily for lacquering the heads on flies, but it can also be used in various steps during the tying process. Veniard's Cellire and the fly-tying head cement sold by Angler's Corner, LaPine, Oregon, are very fine products. Ordinary clear nail polish with nylon is also excellent.

Tying Thread

I recommend that you get thread that is manufactured specifically for fly tying. Unknown brands or dime-store thread are definitely not suitable for serious fly tying. I have used Danville's Herb Howard prewaxed thread for a long time, and have found that none other is needed. It is a very thin size 6/0 but has the strength of the regular 3/0 of other brands. In addition to this fine, thin thread, which you should have in black, white, cream, yellow, red, claret, primrose, brown and orange, one should have a small supply of heavier thread in sizes A to D in black and brown for the spinning of deer hair for muddler heads, and occasionally for ribbing on nymphs.

Wax

Even though the tying thread I have recommended is already prewaxed, there are times when some extra waxing is necessary, particularly when you are working with such materials as seal's fur.

Body Material

Floss

Floss is used for bodies on many of our popular flies. It is a ribbon-type stock and comes in a heavy single strand or several thin ones wound on the spool together, which in turn can be separated and used on smaller flies. It is available in either silk or rayon. Your supplier has a complete list of different colors in stock.

Tinsel

If you intend to tie a lot of streamers and bucktails, you will need some flat tinsel for the bodies, both in wide, medium, and narrow stock. This can also be used for ribbing, but it is best to get some oval and round tinsel for that purpose. All the tinsel comes in either silver or gold.

Lead Wire

This is most often used for adding extra weight to your flies. It's a very soft wire and comes in heavy, medium, and fine diameter. The wire should be chosen to fit the size fly you are tying. The following suggestions may help you choose the right size.

Heavy:	(.031)	fly sizes 6 or larger
Medium:	(.016)	fly sizes 8 to 12
Fine:	(.010)	fly sizes 14 or smaller

Chenille

Even though chenille is not used on very many of the flies, there are some streamers and woolly worms on which it is needed. It is available in many diameters and colors, and looks very much like an ordinary pipe cleaner. The fuzzy material is spun on a silk core and is easy to wind. A good selection should include some in black, white, yellow, red, green, orange, and blue.

Wool Yarn

The water-absorbing qualities of ordinary yarn make it ideally suited for wet flies and nymphs. It comes in every color one can imagine, and most material suppliers have a good stock of wool especially selected for fly tying.

Poly Yarn

This material has been on the market for some time and is widely used for bodies on dry flies when used as a dubbing. It is also available in strands for wings on some of the spinners.

Spectrum Blend

This is a fine synthetic dry-fly blend that is available in fifty different shades; it is excellent whenever a pattern calls for fur dubbing.

Seal-Ex Dubbing

Since baby seals are on the Endangered Species List, their highly sought-after fur has become scarce. Modern technology, however, has made it possible to produce a substitute with a fine sheen and translucency. Seal-Ex is easy to dub and comes in sets of eighteen colors selected especially for fly tying, or preblended in single colors for specific insect imitations that are to be fished under water.

Latex

This is a rubber material used for making segmented bodies on caddis larva and pupa. Also, I use latex for the wing cases of my large black stonefly nymph. It comes from the supplier in five-by-five-inch sheets that can easily be cut into strips with your scissors, a razor blade, or simply cut on a paper cutter. The medium and heavy-duty stock give you the best results. Latex can be dyed any color or tinted with a waterproof marking pen after the fly is finished.

Natural Furs

Whenever possible, I use the natural fur for dry-fly bodies; by blending it with other fur that has been dyed I am usually able to come up with the shade that a particular pattern calls for. Small pieces of skin can be purchased from your supplier, and by looking through his catalog you can make a suitable selection. The most commonly used are these from the following animals:

> *Fox:* gray, tan, fawn, cream, and the pinkish belly fur
> *Opossum:* black, gray, light tan, and creamy yellow
> *Otter:* creamish gray
> *Beaver:* brownish to blue gray
> *Muskrat:* blue to blue gray
> *Mole:* the bluest blue gray
> *Hare's Ear:* rusty brown to dark gray
> *Squirrel:* substitute for hare's ear
> *Rabbit:* brown to dark-gray shades—white skins dyed in many
>   different colors
> *Seal:* natural cream to pale amber—also dyed in various colors

Hackle

Being able to recognize the various shades and quality of hackle and applying it to the proper uses is very important for the fly tyer. Whenever a fly is designed to be fished on the surface, one naturally selects the stiffest hackle available so it will support the weight of the fly and keep it floating while fishing. For wet flies I prefer to use a hen hackle which is much softer and, therefore, livelier under water. For streamer wings it is best to use saddle hackle. They have some very "springy" stems and fibers on the tip portions and some full webby portions at the base, which makes them ideally suited for "lively" wings. The following descriptions of the various hackles you will need can be used for identifying dry-fly necks, as well as saddle patches and hen necks when ordering your supplies.

> *White:* natural white to creamy white
> *Black:* natural black or dyed
> *Cream:* often found among the white necks
> *Light Ginger:* these necks have a pale tan shade
> *Dark Ginger:* a brown to light-brown shade
> *Coachman Brown:* the feathers on this neck are mahogany brown
> *Natural Red:* a brown to reddish-brown shade—very popular
> *Coch-y-Bondhu:* dark brown with black edges and tip
> *Furnace:* brown to medium-brown with a black center—excellent for streamer wings
> *Badger:* white to creamy-white with black center stripe; like the furnace, this is a very good streamer hackle
> *Blue Dun:* light to dark blue-gray shade; some necks appear to be almost black
> *Grizzly:* often called Plymouth Rock; the hackles are gray and black barred; sometimes they are also available in multi-color (ginger, gray and brown) in which case they are referred to as "multi-variant" hackle.

The above list is by no means conclusive, and there are many shades of necks that are nearly impossible to describe though they are sometimes important. I urge you to go through a barrel of necks whenever you see one. Who knows? You may find just what you are looking for.

Body hackles

> *Partridge:* these are gray with delicate brown markings—excellent for legs on many of the most useful nymphs
> *Grouse:* dark brown spotted with tan; like the partridge, they are used mostly for legs on nymphs and wet flies
> *Guinea Hen:* very dark gray to black with white "polka dots" or "speckles"

Wing Material

Feathers

> *Duck:* white, gray, and slate-gray primary wing quills; (pointers) natural or dyed in various colors

Goose: dark gray and natural white primary or secondary wing quills, natural or dyed—well suited for larger flies

Crow: black to metallic-black wing quills

Turkey: brown-mottled secondary wing quills for flies like the Muddler Minnow; the tails are very dark brown-mottled, some with white tips

Marabou: soft fluffy white or dyed any color; well suited for streamer wings

Wood Duck: the lemon-colored flank feathers are used for wings on such flies as the Quill Gordon and Hendrickson, both wet and dry

Teal: the flank feathers are well-marked with light gray and black bars

Mallard: the body and flank feathers are whitish-gray with medium gray barring

Ring Neck Pheasant: the tails on this bird are very useful. Short tail feathers are used for wing cases on nymphs, and the fibers from the center tail are the most sought-after for tails on many of the popular nymphs. Some of the well-marked body feathers can be used for cut wings on dry flies.

Hair

Squirrel Tail: a popular hair for streamer wings. The most common is the gray tail with white hair-tips, and the fox squirrel, which is reddish-brown with black tips.

Calf Tail: used for wings on both streamers, wet, and dry flies. It is a white, brown, or black crinkled hair that is normally used on larger flies.

Black Bear: a rather coarse black to brownish hair

Polar Bear: very fine translucent and shiny white to creamy-white hair. Used mostly for streamers. This hair can also be dyed in any color.

Bucktail: these tails are very popular for wings on the flies bearing the name. It is a rather long white hair with a natural tan to dark blackish-brown hair in the middle outside of the tail. It can be dyed any color.

Mink: the guard hairs from the tail of these small animals are often used for wings on caddis dry flies. They can be obtained in natural tan to brown, or dyed any color.

Deer Hair: the hollow hair from the hides of deer are not used very often as whole wings but for spinning the collar and heads on flies like the Muddler Minnow. They are also used as part of the wings on such terrestrials as hoppers and beetles.

2

GETTING STARTED

IF IT WAS LEFT UP TO THE FLY TYER, I'M SURE THE LARGEST ROOM IN the house would be reserved for just fly tying. It most cases, however, one must settle for a desk in the den or the kitchen table where we can clamp the vise if it is not on a stand of some sort.

In addition to the vise there should be enough space to set a small high-intensity lamp and for laying out the various tools and other sundries you need. Aside from those essentials, it is practical to attach a small scrap bag in front of you at the vise. These bags can be purchased from your supplier at very little cost and will enable you to keep a clean and orderly work area. Finally, the six-by-eight-inch cardboard held in a pair of hemostats and located eight to ten inches behind the vise serves as a background against which the various materials show up better and ease the strain on your eyes when you focus on the hook. I use different colored cardboard for better contrast with the shades of material being used.

18

A simple fly-tying setup

This may look like a simple setup—and it is. But you should always bear in mind that it's not the amount of room or the amount of money spent that make a master: it's *practice*.

FLY TYING BASICS

Regardless of the type of fly you have decided to tie, there are some basic steps that are always the same, such as placing the hook in the vise and attaching the tying thread. Over the years I have seen many different ways of doing this; since most of them work, I have come to the conclusion that one should use the way that seems most comfortable, as long as it is practical. Some tyers, for example, prefer to bury the entire bend and hook-point in the vise-jaws so that the sharp point doesn't cut the tying thread by accident; others just place the hook in the jaws by a small portion of the bend, leaving the hook-point exposed. I use the latter method for several reasons. First, the hook-shank is freer from the tip of the jaws; second, the point and barb are often used as a point of reference when you attach the various materials. With practice you will soon learn to manipulate around the hook-point.

Attaching the Tying Thread

1: Select a bobbin with the desired color thread and release about three to five inches of thread. (For clarity, this technique is shown with a large hook and a piece of fly line.)

Hold the thread end between your fingers with one hand while holding the bobbin with the other so the short end of the thread is tight. Hold the thread against the near side of the hook-shank at an angle. The portion of the shank where the tying thread is to be attached may vary from tyer to tyer, but as a general rule it is at a spot on the shank just inside the hook eye in front. As you learn more about fly tying, or as it may apply to special tying procedures, it can be changed and attached anywhere along the shank.

2: Now take four or five close turns of tying thread in a clockwise direction toward the rear with your bobbin hand, winding it over the thread end, which is being held tight with your fingers on the other hand, thus binding it down on the shank.

3: Cut the surplus thread end close to the windings and your tying thread is attached. In most cases the entire shank will be covered with thread, as explained later during the actual tying instructions; this will form a good foundation on which the various body materials can be applied.

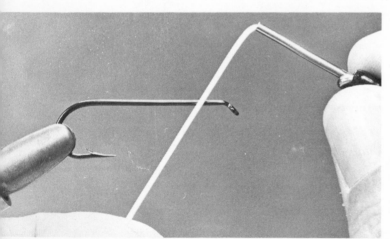

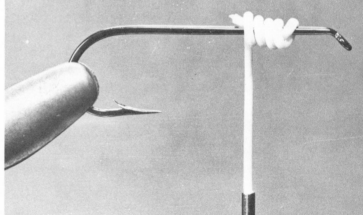

Step 2

Step 1   Step 3

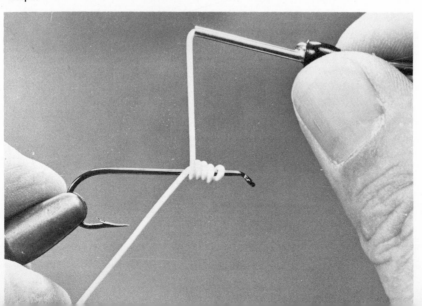

Making a Half Hitch

I do not use the half hitch very much anymore since the weight of the bobbin will usually hold the thread and prevent the windings from unraveling while I prepare materials with my hands. Since there are still some who prefer to tie flies without a bobbin, the half hitch is an important knot to know.

1: Release four to six inches of tying thread between the end of the bobbin and the hook-shank. With the bobbin in your left hand, form a loop around your fingers, making sure the thread leading to the bobbin is on the near side of the end leading to the hook-shank; then position your left index finger where the thread forms a cross, as seen in the photograph.

2: Without moving the thread, locate your left thumb on the thread against the index finger and hold it while sliding the loop over the hook-eye. After that you merely slide the thread loop to the position where you want to locate the half hitch and pull it tight. Some tyers use several half hitches to finish off the thread when the fly is finished, although the whip-finish knot is definitely better.

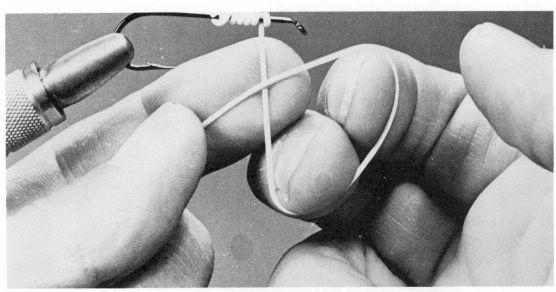

Step 1

Step 2

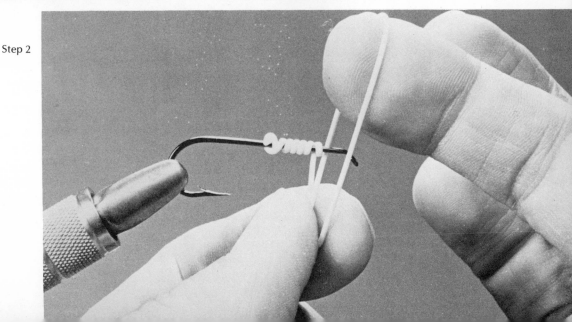

Whip Finishing Knot

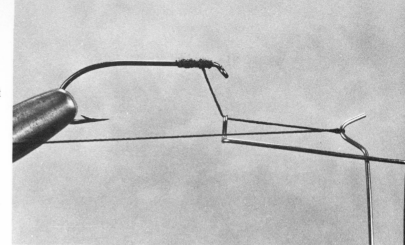

1

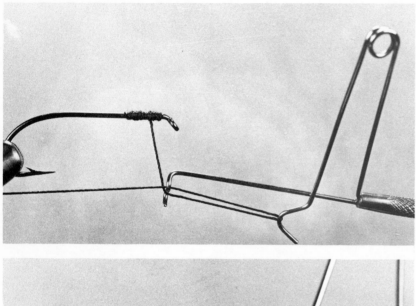

2

3

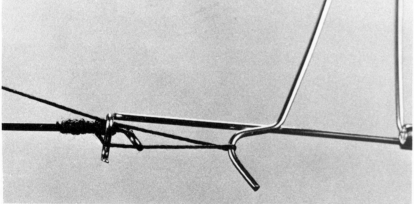

4

3 TYING SOME BASIC FLIES

THE MAYFLY NYMPH

THERE ARE LITERALLY HUNDREDS OF DIFFERENT ARTIFICIAL NYMPHS on record for having taken fish at one time or another, and new ones are being added every year. Most of us, however, manage to select a few representatives that work best in our particular area. The nymphs included in this book were carefully selected to cover a wide range of shapes; I believe they will satisfy all your needs for fishing anywhere in the world.

In spite of all the new artificials that have appeared in the last few years, tied with the newest innovative methods and dressed with the latest synthetics, the old ones are still in use. The oldest and most popular nymph devised as an imitator is still the one that has two or three fibers from the center tail of a cock pheasant tied in to represent the tails, and a body of genuine fur that is ribbed with tinsel or thread.

The legs are imitated by a hackle palmered over the front one third of the body, over which there is a quill section tied flat to imitate the wing case. Many of our most famous nymphs are dressed exactly in that manner, and only the material used makes the difference between one and another.

The following tying instructions are therefore important and should be learned well so you can tie most of the favorite patterns. As a guideline, I have chosen the American March Brown; the material list is as follows:

HOOK:	size 10 (Mustad #9671)
THREAD:	brown
TAIL:	pheasant fibers
BODY:	amber seal and red fox—brown rib
THORAX:	none
LEGS:	brown partridge
WING CASE:	pheasant tail

1: Place the hook in the vise and attach the tying thread as explained in the chapter "Getting Started." Cover the hook-shank with tying thread as you wind it to the bend, where the three fibers from a cock pheasant center tail are tied in. They should project about a hook's length beyond the bend for this particular nymph.
2: If you wish to weight your nymph, the lead wire should be applied now—usually some .010 lead wire occupying the middle one third of the shank. After applying the lead wire I generally cover it with tying thread and apply a little tying cement.

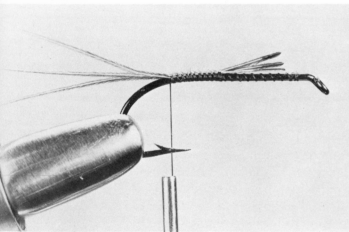

Step 1

Step 2

3: Tie in a four-inch length of brown button-hole silk or similar heavy thread at the bend where the tail was tied in. Mix some amber seal's fur and the red-fox belly fur, then dub it on the tying thread by rolling it on with your fingers. Try to make a nice taper, as seen in the photograph.
4: Apply a little cement on the hook-shank and wind the body fur to

Step 3

Step 4

just slightly past the middle of the hook, followed by the brown ribbing which is spiralled forward to the same position and tied off. Cut the surplus end and peel off any excess fur dubbing from the tying thread. Now tie in a three-sixteenths-inch wide quill strip taken from the short tail feather of a cock pheasant. This is tied in with the good side up, so later, when it is folded over, the underside will show. Sometimes I first spray the quill segment with clear lacquer so that it won't split.

5: Now tie in a small brown partridge body hackle directly in front of the finished body portion and dub the front of the body in the same manner as you did the rear but without the ribbing. The longest fibers on the partridge feather should be about the same size as the distance from the hook-eye to the hook-point.

6: Spiral the partridge feather open palmer style over the front body portion and tie it off in front. Cut the surplus and fold the quill strip forward over the body, while dividing the partridge fibers evenly to each side. Tie down the quill section in front, close to the eye, with several tight turns, then trim away the surplus quill. To finish the fly, wind a small head and tie off the thread with a whip-finishing knot or some half hitches.

Step 5

Step 6

STONE-FLY NYMPHS

I don't think there is any other aquatic nymph that has stronger or more recognizable features than the natural stone fly. The artificial, however, is dressed much in the same way, and using the same tying technique as was used for the mayfly nymph. The major difference is found in the construction of the wing case. The mayfly nymph has a single case, whereas the stone fly nymph has two. To accomplish this the first quill strip is tied on in the same manner as explained in Step 4 for tying the mayfly nymph, but instead of folding the quill section forward it is doubled over a dubbing needle at the desired length and tied down at the same spot where it was first tied in. When that is done, apply a turn or two of dubbing to cover the thread windings, then tie in the second quill section just slightly in front of the first one. Now tie in the feather you have selected to represent the legs and dub the remainder of the body almost to the hook-eye. Wind the hackle legs and tie off in front. Double the second quill section and tie it down in front. Separate a fiber on each side of the surplus quill end to serve as the two antennae and trim away the rest, leaving some short stumps to represent the head. Whip finish, apply some lacquer on the windings, and the stone fly nymph is finished.

Latex Wing Cases

In recent years, or since latex material has found its way into fly tying, I have used it for imitating the wing cases on stone-fly nymphs. I prefer the heavy stock for this type of work because it is easier to handle and sits better when tied in. A stone fly with such wing cases is illustrated in the photograph together with a set of the wings trimmed to shape. The cone-shaped segment also illustrated is tied in front after the wing cases are attached to represent the pronotum, which is sitting between the head and the first wing case. When the nymph is finished, the latex is tinted with a waterproof marking pen to match the shade of the rest of the nymph.

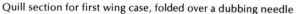

Quill section for first wing case, folded over a dubbing needle

A finished stone-fly nymph

Latex wing cases and a Jorgensen Latex Stone-Fly Nymph

CADDIS PUPA AND LARVA

The natural caddis pupa and larva vary considerably from may flies and stone flies both in appearance and development; to some degree the artificials are also dressed differently. The caddis larva is a slim cylindrical wormlike insect with a dirty-colored abdomen and a dark blackish-brown thorax. They can be dressed either with a fur or latex body, which in most cases should be weighted with some lead wire before the body is applied so they will sink down to where the fish are looking for them. The thorax is a very small portion in front dubbed with fur from which the legs can be picked out underneath. They are among the easiest flies to tie. The pupa, however, is not that simple; it is quite difficult to imitate successfully because of the natural's high translucency. I prefer to make the abdomen with Seal-Ex, which, when wet, is very translucent. The simple instructions that follow can be used for dressing most of the caddis pupa you will ever need.

Latex Caddis Larva

1: Form the rear portion of the body, starting midway down on the bend on a Mustad hook #3906. Since the pupa is to be fished deep it's best to add some lead wire on the shank before the body is applied. If you wish, the fur can be spun in a loop before it is wound, or simply dubbed directly on the thread. If the body is to be ribbed with either thread or tinsel, that material must be attached before the body is applied like the ribbing for the March Brown may-fly nymph explained earlier. Next, prepare two sections of grey duck wing quill, spraying them with a clear lacquer like Krylon. Tie in a strip on each side of the finished body portion.

This brings you to the front of the body, legs and head, which can be dressed in several different ways. The Solomon type of pupa uses a small bunch of fibers from a partridge hackle tied under in the front like a "beard," with a couple of fibers on top to represent the antennae; the front of the pupa is finished with a couple of turns of peacock herl. The Jorgensen style, however, requires the legs and thorax portion to be dressed in one application, using guard hair and underfur from the back of a rabbit. This is done as follows after finishing step one.

2: Cut a thin layer of fur and guard hair from the back of a rabbit that has been dyed dark brown.

Step 1   Step 2

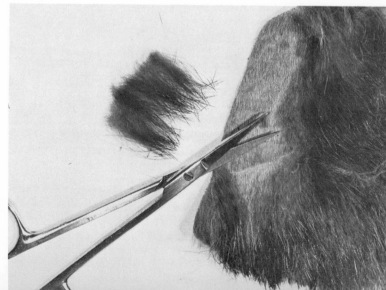

3: Form a three-inch spinning loop in front of the finished body portion of the pupa and insert the fur as seen in the photograph. Make sure the fur and guard hair are not mixed up, but are inserted well spread out—as they were cut from the skin.

4: Place a pair of heavy hackle pliers in the end of the loop and spin a fur "chenille."

5: Moisten your fingers a little and stroke the fur and guard hair back as it is being wound like a doubled wet-fly hackle. Tie it off in front, cut the surplus, and trim the top and side fur a little, but leave all of it underneath to represent the legs. When trimming the top, try to leave a few hairs to imitate the antennae. The fly is finished off with a small head of tying thread, which should be lacquered.

Step 3

Step 5

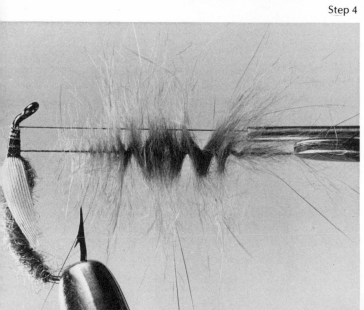

Step 4

THE DRY FLY

May-fly imitations are still first on the fly fisher's list, followed closely by caddis flies and landborn insects like grasshoppers, crickets, ants, and beetles, plus a variety of smaller, minute insects of importance both to the fish and the angler. But regardless of what the artificials are imitating they all have one thing in common: they must float so they can be fished on the surface, and a great deal of care must be exercised when picking the various materials that go into them. Unfortunately, it's quite beyond the scope of this book to go deeply into all the mysteries of the dry fly, but there are some very basic techniques that are used for dressing many of the most popular patterns. Careful study of the following instructions will enable you to tie a decent dry fly that will catch fish almost anywhere.

The May-Fly Imitation

I have chosen the Grizzly Wulff as a model for the instructions as it is not only a good fish getter but also a rather large fly that is of typical dry-fly construction. To tie it you need the following material:

HOOK:	size 6 to 16
THREAD:	black
TAIL:	brown calf tail
BODY:	pale yellow floss, lacquered
WING:	brown calf tail
HACKLE:	brown and grizzly

1: Tie in a small bunch of hair on top of the hook, right at the bend. Make sure it's long enough to project one hook length beyond the bend with the butt ends reaching to about the middle of the hook.
2: Take another bunch of hair, twice as much as for the tail, and tie it in on the shank one third of a hook length from the eye. The hair tips should project forward over the eye of the hook and be as long as the tail, measuring from the tie-in windings to the hair tips.
3: Trim the butt ends of the wing material to a taper so it blends well with the butts from the tail, then wind the tying thread over both to form a smooth-tapered underbody. Now grasp all the wing hair and raise it to a ninety degree angle and wind some tying thread directly in front of, and tightly against, the wing hair. Divide the hair into two bunches of the same size and criss cross the tying thread between them until they are firmly fastened. Apply a little cement on the windings to secure them.
4: Tie in some floss and wind a smooth body that reaches almost to the wing position, then tie in the hackles as seen in the photograph. The length of the hackle fibers should be about a hook gap and a half.
5: Wind the hackles one at a time, taking the first turn of the first hackle around the shank at the tie-in spot, and the second turn tightly up against the back of the wing; take the first turn in front

Step 1

Step 2

Step 3

Step 4

Step 5

tightly up against the front of the wing, then wind some extra turns forward to the eye and tie it off. The second hackle is then wound through the first one to the same place in front and tied off. Wind a small head and apply cement. When the fly is finished, the yellow floss body is given a thin coat of clear lacquer to protect it from the fish's teeth.

Other Body and Wing Styles

While the Grizzly Wulff was designed with a body of floss and the wings and tail of hair, there are other dry flies, just as effective, that are dressed with other types of material. Peacock herl, for example, is used for bodies either stripped of all the flues for a segmented effect, or wound whole as they come. The Quill Gordon is a good example of a body with stripped peacock herl. Fur is also used, either natural or synthetic, which can be seen on the Isonychia Cut-Wing fly. At the same time, the two flies illustrate two different wing styles. The Quill Gordon is dressed with a wood-duck flank feather wing, and the Isonychia has wings trimmed to shape from two rooster body feathers. These can be trimmed with your scissors or a pair of heavy toenail clippers.

Spent-Wing May Flies

This type of fly, also called spinners, is the second stage of a may-fly adult. The wings are now glassy clear and can be well imitated by very pale dun-colored poly-yarn or hackle tips. You can use the same tying instructions given for the ordinary dry fly with upright wings, except that the wings are tied spent and are extended out from the body like the wings on an airplane. The material list for the various patterns will indicate the type of wing material to use.

Caddis Dry Flies

Because of the publicity awarded to this insect in the last few years, caddis flies have become an important part of an angler's fly box. The insects, of course, have been around all the time, but no one had bothered to separate them from all the rest of the stream insects the fly tyer tried to imitate, and ordinary dry flies were used with more or less adequate success. But now they are treated differently, and specific patterns have been developed to further cram our fly boxes which are already full. The tying technique for the caddis dry fly is not much different from that of the ordinary dry fly explained earlier, with the obvious exceptions that the tail has been omitted, the wing is tied down instead of upright, and the hackle is wound in front after the wing is attached.

Terrestrials (Landborn Insects)

There are always days on the trout stream when one fly seems to work better than the other. It could be because of the water level, the time of year, or simply because there is an abundance of one type of natural

Hen Spinner

Left. Quill Gordon with a quill body and a wood-duck wing. *Right:* a Cut-wing Parachute Dun with a fur body and wings trimmed to shape.

Caddis Hair-wing Fly

Terrestrials. *Top row:* Whitlock Hopper. *Below, left to right:* Inchworm, Black Beetle, and Jassid.

insect and very few of all the rest. When I think of terrestrials, I nearly always think of Pennsylvania's streams, and Letort Spring Creek, where Vince Marinaro and Charles Fox refined to a science the method of fishing with imitations of grasshoppers, crickets, beetles, ants, and many other of the smaller creatures found in the meadows along this storied creek. Like the caddis flies, one can use more or less the same tying instructions given earlier for dressing the ordinary dry fly and look at the photographs of the various insects you are tying. The head and part of the wing you see on the hopper and cricket are spun deer hair that is trimmed to shape after it is wound on the hook. The method of spinning the hair is the same as is used for the muddler head explained under "The Streamer"; only the trimming and shaping of the hair is different.

THE WET FLY

Everyone who fishes for trout seems to have some kind of favorite wet fly that he fishes with most of the time. I remember a trip to Kettle Creek in Pennsylvania a few years ago, when my friends Bob Byron and Frank Chaplin invited me to fish with a fellow named Larry Cartwright who was supposed to be some kind of master with the wet fly. When Larry was guiding me around to his favorite spots, I noticed that he turned his back to me every time he changed his fly—as if he didn't want me to see what he was using. It wasn't the secrecy about the flies that upset me, but the fact that he was outfishing me four to nothing. When I couldn't stand it any more and politely asked him what he was using, he turned to me and grinned. "Look at Byron's hatband," he said; "that will give you a clue." Both Bob and Frank had hatbands lined with Hendrickson wet flies in every size you can imagine. "You see," Larry said, "all I did with my back to you was change the size." Friends sometimes act funny when they are one up on you—particularly fishing friends.

Wet flies were designed to imitate the many winged insects that for one reason or another are found under water in the stream, like hatching may flies, diving caddis flies, and caddis pupa. The later was undoubtedly the one Larry's fish were taking, and the Hendrickson is a very good imitator to use when subsurface caddis are active, even though specific patterns for imitating the pupa are now on the "best seller" list.

To tie a wet fly one can again use the basic instructions given earlier for tying the dry fly, except for he hackle and wing. The pattern I have chosen is the Dark Hendrickson.

Material List

HOOK:	size 10 to 14
THREAD:	black
TAIL:	blue dun
BODY:	grey fur
HACKLE:	blue dun
WING:	wood-duck flank feather

1: After tying in the tail and body as explained earlier in the sections dealing with nymphs and dry flies, select a blue dun hackle with the longest fibers about as long as the distance between the eye and the hookpoint. Stroke down the fibers so that they stand out from the stem at a right angle, then trim away the fibers a quarter of an inch up each side of the stem at the tip end of the feather, leaving only some small stumps. Tie it in as seen in the photograph, with the good side up.

Wind hackle in front of the body, either doubling the fibers back, or stroking them back, before each turn. Three or four turns should suffice. Tie off the hackle and trim away the surplus, making sure there is a small space left in front for the wing, which is tied in next.

Step 1   Step 2

Step 3

Different wet-fly styles. *Top row, left to right.*
The Starling Herl, Morse's Alder fly.
Bottom: Dark Stone

2: Strip the fuzz and unwanted fibers from the base of a wood-duck flank feather that is long enough in the fibers for the size fly you are tying. Leave enough fibers on each side of the stem to give you a feather that is about twice as long as the hook length measured from the tip and down. Gather all the fibers together and tie them in as a bunch while they are still sitting on the stem. The fibers should sit not only on top, but expand a little down on each side without flaring out. I sometimes moisten the fibers a little with my fingers to manipulate them better. The tips of the wing fibers should extend just slightly beyond the bend of the hook.

3: Trim the surplus feather and wind the head, then apply a little cement and the wet fly is finished.

Other Wing Styles

Sometimes wet flies—like Tup's Indispensable, The Starling Herl and other "soft hackle" flies—are tied with no wings at all. But in addition to the flank feather wing that is used on several of our favorite flies, there are some that are dressed with wings of hair and others that are dressed with wings of quill. The hair wing is tied on as a bunch like the flank feather, but the quill wings are a little different and will require a technique that is explained in the following instructions. For these you can tie up a body as explained in the instructions for the Hendrickson, using Steps 1 and 2.

1: Select two mallard primary wing feathers, one from the left wing and one from the right. Cut a quill section of the same size from each of the wing feathers as seen in the photograph. They should be about as wide as two thirds of the hook-gap. The feather section to the left will form the right (near) wing and the right section will form the left (far) wing.

2: Place the two strips together, back-to-back, with the tips curving against each other and slightly up. Align the tips and hold them over the body with your left hand at a low horizontal position. You can separate the butt ends a little and lower the segments slightly, keeping the body between them. This will enable you to keep them a little down on the side of the hook when they are fastened.

3: Now take your tying thread straight up between the near quill strip and the tip of your thumb. Hold it there while bringing the tying thread over both quill strips and down on the other side between the far strip and your index finger, and continue to complete the turn by going under the hook and again up between the strip and your thumb on the near side. When the turn is completed, hold the tying thread up above the wings and press both quill strips tightly between your fingers while pulling the thread loop tight with an upward pull. Take a couple of extra turns to securely fasten the wing.

4: Trim the surplus and wind the head. Apply a little cement on the thread windings and your fly is finished.

Step 1

Step 2

Step 3

Step 4

THE STREAMER FLY

Streamers are not really flies but imitations of the many different bait-fish found in our rivers and ponds. As they are usually fished with a fly rod, I suppose it was fitting to refer to them as flies. These artificials are generally divided into two groups with a distinct difference in character: some are called streamers and others bucktails.

The streamer for the most part is dressed with a wing consisting of two or more neck or saddle hackles tied in on top of a body dressed on a long shank hook. The bucktail, on the other hand, may use the same type body, but the wing is made from the hair of a deer's tail that is either natural or dyed in different colors. However, it's not unusual to find patterns with wings that are made up of a combination of the two, in which case they are most often referred to as streamers. There are other variations, such as the Muddler Minnow, the Matuka, and the Sculpin; these are usually called those names rather than either bucktails or streamers.

A simple streamer is fairly easy to tie. I have chosen the famous Black Ghost as a model for your tying, not only because of its simple construction but because it's noted for being a very effective fly when all others fail.

Material list:

HOOK:	2 to 12, 6X long
THREAD:	black
TAIL:	yellow hackle fibers
BODY:	black floss, silver ribbing
THROAT:	yellow hackle fibers
WING:	four white hackles
CHEEKS:	jungle cock

1: Tie in a small bunch of yellow-dyed hackle fibers at the bend to represent the tail, together with a six-inch length of flat ribbing tinsel that is fastened underneath. The tail fibers should be about as long as one-and-a-half hook gaps. Now wind the tying thread forward to one-eighth inch from the eye and tie in a length of black floss that is long enough to be wound to the tail and then back over the first layer to the tie-in spot.

2: Wind the floss and ribbing as seen, then tie it off in front and cut the surplus. Now tie in a small bunch of yellow-dyed hackle fibers about as long as the tail. These will represent the throat and are fastened under the shank.

3: Prepare four white saddle hackles for the wing. It's best to select them from a whole saddle to get the right size and curvature. Measure the length, which when tied in should reach half a body length past the hook-bend. Trim a few fibers off each side of the stem at the butt-ends so they will not slip out after they are tied in. As you can see in the photograph, the feathers are laid out in pairs with matching curvatures and their good sides up. The pair to the left will form the far (left) wing and the other, for obvious reasons,

Step 1

Step 2

Step 3

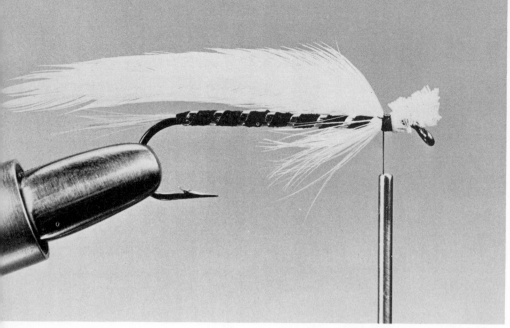

Step 4

will form the one nearest to you. Now place one feather in each pair on top of the other and put the two pairs together to form a wing as seen in the photograph. There should be a good side out on each side of the wing.

4: Tie in the wing as seen, fastening all four hackles at the same time with the stems lying side by side.

5: Trim the surplus and tie in the jungle cock cheeks, one on each side. Wind a nice tapered head and apply some black lacquer.

Step 5

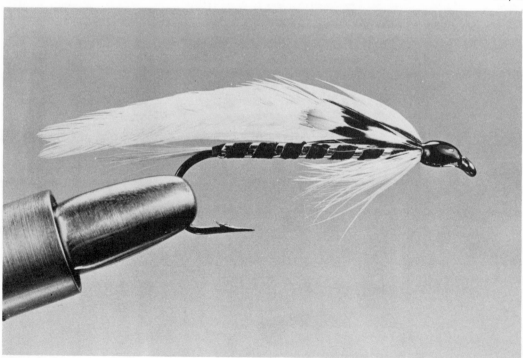

Two bucktail streamers: Warden's Worry *(left)* and Esopus

Bucktails

The bodies for most bucktails are not very different from those used for the streamer. The bucktail itself should be of modest quantity, either of one single color as seen in the Warden's Worry or layers of several colors as is the case for the wing on the Esopus. I usually apply a little cement on the butt-ends of the bucktail and taper them in front so a nice tapered head can be wound. Other than that, one can use the same tying instructions that I have given throughout the previous sections of the book.

The Muddler Minnow

The Muddler Minnow is the best known of all the streamer-type flies in existence. It was designed by Don Gapen of Anoka, Minnesota, while on a fishing trip to the Nipigon River in Canada. Since then it has been used as a model for many variations, including the Marabou Muddler, the Sculpin, the Streaker, and many many others. It is sad, however, that today's Muddler doesn't look much like the one Don Gapen designed because today's tyers dress the head so packed with deer hair that it's almost impossible to sink the fly. Unless the Muddler is intended for surface fishing, I would suggest you study the following instructions; they will show you how to tie the Muddler head and collar with just one application of hair, and also the proper method of trimming the head.

Material list
HOOK: 2 to 12, 4X long
THREAD: brown
TAIL: mottled turkey
BODY: flat gold tinsel
WING: squirrel tail and mottled turkey
COLLAR: deer-body hair
HEAD: deer-body hair, trimmed

1: Tie in the tail, body, and wing using the material list given and the tying instructions explained for tying the wet flies and feather streamer. Note that I have left about three sixteenths of an inch in front for the collar and head. This may seem like a rather small space, but that's all you need for a one-application Muddler head.

2: Tie off the thin thread you used for tying up until now, and attach some heavy size A thread securely, directly in front of the wing. The thread should be well waxed, and must under no circumstances be allowed to slip when being wound and pulled tight to flair the hair. Cut a bunch of deer-body hair about the size of a lead pencil in diameter when lightly compressed and brush out all the fuzz from the butt-ends. Now tie in the hair as seen and pull the tying thread tight. The tips of the hair collar should reach to a little past the middle of the wing, and the butt ends should be about a half inch long. The tying thread is now wound through the hair butts to the front, where it is tied off. Each turn you take through the hair must be pulled tight so the hair will flair out each time. Three or four spiraled turns will usually suffice.

3: Now trim the head with your scissors from behind. As you can see, the hair is trimmed almost flush with the underside of the body and the top and sides are trimmed to blend with the wing.

Step 1

Step 2

Step 3

4

POUL JORGENSEN'S TYING TIPS

THE FOLLOWING INFORMATION WILL SUPPLEMENT THE RECIPES GIVEN for all flies shown in the color section. A special section on the very newest flies is given at the end.

NYMPHS

81 **BAETIS NYMPH** Usually tied on Mustad #9671 hook. The size of this fly decreases as the season progresses. The body is a mixture of beaver and red fox.

81 **BITCH CREEK NYMPH** Usually tied on Mustad #3665A or #9575 hook. Care should be taken when weaving the chenille. The orange must be on the bottom and the black kept on top. A fine white rubber band can be cut up for tails and feelers.

81 **BLUE QUILL NYMPH** I use Mustad hook #9671 for this fly. A soft ginger cock hackle can be substituted for

legs. Dyed black goose can be substituted for wing case.

81 **BLUE-WINGED OLIVE NYMPH** My preference is a Mustad #9671 hook. The body fur is blended from beaver and red fox.

81 **CADDIS LARVA, Olive** I use either Mustad #3906 or #3906B hooks. The body is pale olive rabbit fur with a touch of gray underfur to give it a dirty olive shade. The collar can be either fur, mini-ostrich or peacock herl.

81 **CADDIS LARVA, White** Use same hook as above. Blend white rabbit with a touch of gray for a dirty white body color.

Pattern colors can be varied to match local caddis larva.

81 **CADDIS PUPA, Brown** I use either Mustad #3906 or #3906B hook. To make the abdomen portion I start by forming a spinning loop midway down the bend of the hook. Dyed rabbit mixed with seal or fox is best. Spin it tight to a ropelike dubbing so it will make a segmented effect when wound on. For the wings I use the primary wing quills or the shoulder feathers. In both cases they should be sprayed with Krylon to prevent splitting. Thorax and legs are formed in one operation by spinning a bunch of underfur with heavy guardhairs still in it. This is taken right from the skin without blending it. Add a few partridge, grouse or woodcock fibers to the guardhairs. When spun it will be like a chenille and can be wound as a wet fly hackle by stroking fur and hair back after each turn. Trim the top and sides to form the thorax, but leave it long underneath to form the legs.

The same procedures given for the Brown Caddis Pupa can be applied to the cream, green and gray Caddis Pupa. The green Caddis Pupa often shades towards olive. There are many local variations in colors.

82 **CAENIS NYMPH, FUR** I use a Mustad #9671 hook. The body should be rather thick, and the fur is blended from bleached Australian opossum and dark red fox. The abdomen is ribbed with fine monocord. The wing case and thorax is made from dyed black rabbit unblended from the skin and spun in a loop. When wound on, it's trimmed off on the bottom and lacquered on top with clear nail polish.

82 **CASUAL DRESS** Use a Mustad hook #9672. The body is dubbed from gray muskrat underfur. The collar is muskrat fur with plenty of guardhair. The fur is unblended as it comes off the skin and spun in a spinning loop, then wound as a wet fly hackle, stroking it back for each turn.

82 **CATSKILL CURLER** I use Mustad hook #79580 for this fly. Start by preparing the wing cases in advance. Select two well marked and evenly matched grouse body feathers. If not available use hen shoulder feathers. Lacquer feathers and trim to shape. Set feathers aside. Using pliers bend hook shank slightly upwards about one third back from eye of hook. Tie in two heavy dark peccary fibers for the tails, each directly on the side of the hook shank. Spread the tails by criss crossing the tying thread. Tie in dyed brown monofilament at the tail and wind thread back to bend in

hook shank. Tie in yellow wool and take a few turns at the bend area to build up under body. Then wind wool back to the tail and taper forward forming an even but thick body. Tie off wool at bend in shank and wind monofilament ribbing up to the wool tie-off point. Tie in another strand of wool and taper towards eye of hook, taking care to leave working space near the eye. Tie in a clump of well barred grouse fibers on the far side of the hook shank and then repeat procedure with another clump on the side nearest you. Secure first wing case directly on top of body. It should slightly extend over the abdomen section of the fly. Tie in the second wing case to cover half of the first wing case. Dub on a collar of dark brown dubbing fur and cover the wing case tie-down area and the remaining space at the hook eye. Tie off fly with a whip finish.

82 **CRESS BUG, FUR** Use Mustad #3906 hook. The entire fly is made by one fur application. Form a spinning loop and insert the fur with guardhairs as it comes off the skin without blending. When it is wound on, trim the top and bottom with your scissors, but leave the fur long on the sides. Apply a little cement on the back, then trim the sides to an oval shape.

82 **DUN VARIANT NYMPH (Flick)** I use a Mustad hook #9671. To make the dubbing, first mix it in a blender, then spin it in a spinning loop and trim lightly to a taper. I sometimes pluck off one side of the grouse feather before winding it on. It's easier to handle that way.

82 **FLEDERMAUS** Use a Mustad hook #9672. The body on this fly is rather

heavy and made from roughly picked out muskrat fur.

82 **GREEN DRAKE** The hook is a Mustad #79580. The tails should be the finest tips from mini-ostrich herl. The mottled turkey used for the wing case is first sprayed with Krylon, then doubled lengthwise. Tie it in at the eye in front of the thorax, with the feather pointing toward the rear. Place your dubbing needle at the desired wing case length and fold the remainder forward over the thorax and tie it off in front. Trim off surplus.

82 **HARE'S EAR, GOLD RIBBED** For this fly I use a Mustad hook #9671 or 3906. I recommend a mixture of hare's ear guardhair and a softer muskrat fur spun in a loop. Gold wire can be used in place of gold tinsel, particularly on small flies. Most of my Hare's Ear flies are weighted.

82 **HELGRAMMITE** Use a Mustad hook #9575. Before the fly is dressed I bend the hook in a slight downward arc as shown in the photograph. Before the body is applied I tie in a piece of lead wire on each side of the shank for weight and to form the oval shape of the abdomen. The lead should be secured tightly with tying thread and cemented. Now tie in a short bunch of brown fibers, a brown saddle hackle fairly long and a wide piece of black raffia for the rib. The body is coarse black and dark brown fur blended and spun in a loop. Wind the dubbing, ribbing and hackle to one-fourth of a hook length from the eye. Trim off hackle fibers top and bottom, then trim side hackle to one body width on each side. Now tie in the turkey

wing case (prepared as in **Green Drake Nymph**) and form a spinning loop. Insert blackish-brown fur aith long guardhairs unblended and spin it, then wind it on front fourth of the hook. Press top fur and hair down to each side and fold the wing case over, leaving excess forward over the eye. To form the mandibles, trim off excess, leaving only two fibers.

82 **HENDRICKSON** Use a Mustad hook #9671. Although the wing case can be tied in and pulled over the thorax (the conventional method), I prefer to prepare and tie the wing case as explained in tying the **Green Drake Nymph.** This more accurately represents the raised wing case of the soon-to-emerge insect.

83 **ISONYCHIA** I prefer a Mustad hook #79580. Partridge, woodcock, and similar feathers can be substituted for legs on this nymph. The wing case can be tied in the same manner as explained above, and is particularly pronounced on this fly.

83 **LEAD-WING COACHMAN** Use a Mustad hook #9672. This fly represents the same insect as the Isonychia above, but is simpler to tie. Unlike the wing case on the above, it's only attached in front and then trimmed to shape like a small wing slip. After tying in the wing slip, the soft hackle is wound as a collar in ordinary wet-fly style.

83 **LEPTOPHLEBIA NYMPH** I prefer a Mustad hook #9672. Before winding the peacock quill it should be well soaked in water or it will break. I sometimes use several quills to cover the abdomen portion.

83 **MARCH BROWN (Flick)** Use a Mustad hook #9671. When tying the tail of three individual fibers (on this or any other nymph with three tails) the center tail is tied first and attached parallel with the hook shank. The other two are then tied in at a 45° angle on each side of the center one. This tail arrangement is particularly pronounced on this nymph. The wing case on Flick's March Brown is attached in front first with the dull side of the feather up. Then it's secured with tying thread behind the thorax and the surplus trimmed away.

83 **MARCH BROWN (Poul's)** For this fly I use a Mustad hook #9671. Wind the body fur to a position a little past the middle of the shank, then tie in the wing case section and the leg hackle. Apply the gray thorax fur and wind the hackle forward. Now pull the wing section forward over the thorax and tie it off. This method is the most conventional way of dressing a nymph.

83 **MICHIGAN MAY FLY, FUR** The best hook is a Mustad #79580. The body fur should be spun in a loop, then clipped top and bottom to give the fly its characteristic flat appearance. When the body is wound and trimmed I give it a light application of cement down the middle on top and pick out the gills on each side. The wing case fur is spun in a loop, wound on and trimmed on the bottom only. The long fur on top I then brush into shape of the wing case with clear cement.

83 **MIDGE PUPA (All Colors)** Use Mustad #94840 or #94842 hook. These are among the simplest flies to tie, and are extremely effective. Besides the gray and cream patterns

shown, olive and black are very popular. Although I tie them very sparse, many tyers prefer them with thick abdomens. Quill bodies are also popular and effective. In the quill-bodied Midge Pupa, I make the head of mini-ostrich herl or thickly spun fur of the color that I want. On fur-bodied midge pupa the head can be either herl or fur of the same color as the body, or simply an extension of the body as shown in the photographs of the gray midge pupa.

83 **MONTANA NYMPH** I prefer a Mustad Hook #79580 or #9672 for this fly. Although the original pattern calls for black crow fiber for the tail, black hackle fibers are often used. As a color variation, I sometimes use brown hackle for tails and legs.

83 **MOSQUITO LARVA** Tie it on a Mustad hook #7957BX. In tying the body, be careful to select one dark and one light moose mane hair for the proper segmented effect. Tie in the grizzly antennae before tying in the thorax.

84 **MUSKRAT NYMPH** I use a Mustad hook #9671. This fly actually represents a caddis larva or pupa and is often tied with a thicker body, roughly dubbed and picked-out. Many fly anglers think, "The uglier the better."

84 **OLIVE DUN** Tied on a Mustad hook #9671. The fur body on this nymph is a blend of medium olive rabbit and light muskrat belly. The gray goose quill wing case is sometimes substituted by one of spun gray fur as in the **Michigan May Fly Nymph.**

84 **OTTER NYMPH** The best hook is a Mustad #9671 or #9672. This fly can also be tied with a thicker body, roughly dubbed and picked-out to get a bushy appearance.

84 **POTAMANTHUS NYMPH** I prefer a Mustad hook #9672. The entire nymph can be made from spun fur of the colors mentioned in the dressing. (See instructions for the **Michigan May Fly Nymph.**) In that case you can use tan fur with plenty of guardhairs for thorax and legs. The fur blend for the body is otter and amber seal, with gills picked-out on each side.

84 **QUILL GORDON NYMPH, FUR** The best hook is Mustad #9671. The abdomen portion of this nymph is a blend of beaver with a touch of light olive seal spun in a loop and trimmed top and bottom for a flat appearance. Rather heavy gills are picked-out on each side. The wing case is dark brown rabbit applied as in the **Michigan May Fly Nymph.**

84 **SHRIMP, FUR** Tied on a Mustad hook #3906. Entire fly is made by one fur application. Form a spinning loop and insert the fur with guardhairs as it comes off the skin without blending. When it is wound, trim the top and both sides with your scissors, but leave the fur long on the bottom forming the legs. Apply a little cement on the back.

84 **STENONEMA, FUR** I use a Mustad hook #9671 or #9672 for this nymph. For the abdomen I blend Australian Opossum with fawn-colored red fox. The wing case is grayish-tan rabbit fur. The entire nymph is tied using the same procedure as for the **Michigan May Fly Nymph.**

84 **STONE FLY, (Poul's)** I use a Mustad hook #79580. Spin the abdomen fur in a loop and wind it on the hook to a little past the middle of the shank, followed by the ribbing. Spray a mottled turkey feather with Krylon and cut two segments and double them lengthwise. Tie in the first feather segment directly in front of the abdomen, with the long end toward the rear and laying flat over the abdomen. Then place your dubbing needle across the feather at the desired length and fold it forward to where it's first tied in, then tie it down with tying thread and cut the surplus. Take a few turns of dubbing fur around the ends and tie in the leg hackle. Wind some more fur forward to one-eighth inch from the eye and spiral the hackle forward in palmer-style and tie it off in front. At the same spot in front, tie in the second wing case and double it like the first one. Be sure the surplus end is fairly long and projecting forward over the eye when the wing case is tied off. Trim away surplus end, leaving two fibers to represent the feelers.

84 **STONE FLY CREEPER (Flick)** The best hook for this nymph is a Mustad #9671 or #9672. After tying-in the tails, wrap a well-soaked and stripped ginger hackle stem on the hook halfway up the shank. Make a spinning loop and spin some amber seal and wind it up to one-eighth inch from the eye and tie off. Tie in the partridge collar. Directly in front of that, tie in a long section of wood duck flank so that it lays flat and projects to the rear and a little beyond. Attach your tying thread at the point where the tail leaves the hook. Hold the wood duck tight to-

ward the rear and tie it down securely. Cut the surplus at the rear and in front, then finish the head. Apply some cement on both sets of windings.

84 **STONE FLY, LARGE BLACK (Poul's)** I use the same hook and tying procedure for this nymph as I used for the **Stone Fly** (Poul's).

85 **SULPHUR NYMPH, FUR** I prefer a Mustad hook #9671 or #3906B. The tying instructions are the same as the **Michigan May Fly Nymph.** The tan fur is blended from bleached Australian Opossum and bleached ginger mink fur.

85 **TELLICO** Tied on a Mustad hook #9671. For this fly I use yellow floss or wool with a peacock herl rib. Wing case should be tied in at the tail and pulled forward after the body has been completed. A popular variation is to use mottled turkey instead of the peacock herl wing case.

85 **ZUG BUG** Use a Mustad Hook #9671 or #9672. A very durable body can be made by laying five or six pieces of the widest peacock herl fibers on the table. Now place a piece of heavy waxed thread on top (it should be the same length as the herl). Grasp the whole bunch and tie it in at the tail. Wind the tying thread forward. Now grasp the end of the herl fibers and heavy waxed thread with your hackle pliers and twist it to a rope-like affair. Wind the herl rope on the shank for the body.

WET FLIES

85 **ALDER** I use a Mustad #9671. If turkey wing quills are not available, the secondary flight feathers from

ringneck pheasants can be used. Furnace hackle can also be used in place of black hen hackle.

85 ALEXANDRA The hook I use is a Mustad #9672. For the tail, tie in three tips of peacock sword. On each side of this goes a narrow strip of dyed red goose quill. Hackle should be tied in as a collar. For the wing, use a larger amount of peacock sword. On each side of the wing carefully tie in a slip of red goose.

85 BEAVERKILL, FEMALE I recommend a Mustad #9671. A soft brown cock hackle can be used in place of brown hen. The egg sac should be tied from the narrowest yellow chenille available. One turn is sufficient. Then tie in the body of gray muskrat in the normal manner.

85 BLACK GNAT Hook can be either Mustad #7957BX or #9671. Black ostrich herl can be used in place of black chenille.

85 BLACK QUILL I prefer using a Mustad hook #9671. Use either stripped peacock quill or a stripped black hackle stem. Be sure to soak well before using or quill will break while being tied in.

85 BLACK WOOLLY WORM I use a Mustad hook #9671 or #9672. Use either a saddle hackle or large neck hackle for palmering. Both badger and furnace are often used in place of grizzly hackle.

85 BLUE DUN I recommend a Mustad hook #9671. The body is of gray muskrat fur, and the collar can be of hen or softest cock hackle available.

86 BLUE WING OLIVE I use a Mustad hook #9671 or #9672. For the body of this fly I use either rabbit, beaver or mink dyed medium olive.

86 BREADCRUST For the hook I recommend a Mustad #9671. Either orange wool or floss can be used for the body. Take great care in preparing the stripped quill rib, and soak well in water before using. After tying off the quill, wrap a collar of the softest grizzly hackle (wet fly style).

86 BROWN HACKLE I use a Mustad hook #9671. After tying in a silk tail, pick out silk until all fibers are single strands. Wool can be used in place of silk. For the body, select widest peacock herl (just below the eye on the tail feather). Wrap the collar of softest brown hackle.

86 BROWN WOOLLY WORM I use a Mustad hook #9671 or #9672. Use either a saddle or large neck hackle for palmering. As a substitute for grizzly hackle you can use either furnace or badger.

86 CAHILL, DARK I prefer either a Mustad hook #9671 or #9672. The tail is of brown hackle fibers. For the body I use the darkest gray muskrat I can find. The wing is a bunch of wood duck flank fibers. If wood duck is not available, use a substitute of Mallard flank dyed the shade of wood duck.

86 CAHILL, LIGHT Use a Mustad hook, either #9671 or #9672. The tail is traditionally tied from several fibers of wood duck flank, but several light ginger hackle fibers may be substituted. I use cream red fox belly for the body, but bleached raccoon or bleached Australian Opossum may be used. The wing can be either wood duck flank or mallard flank dyed wood duck.

86 **CAREY SPECIAL** I use either a Mustad #7957BX or #9671 hook. The body is medium-size brown chenille. Rib should be medium or large oval tinsel, depending on the size of the fly. Strip the fluff off the flank feather of a cock pheasant and wind hackle as a collar.

86 **CLARET GNAT** I use either a Mustad #9671 or #7957BX hook. Use either hen hackle or softest cock hackle dyed claret. After tying in the hackle collar, set wings directly on top of hook shank over the collar.

86 **COACHMAN** Use a Mustad hook #9671. Select the widest possible herl available for the body. The wing can be either white duck or white goose primary flight feathers. Tie in wings after coachman or dark brown hackle collar is wound on.

86 **COACHMAN, CALIFORNIA** I use a Mustad hook, #9671 or #9672, for this fly. This fly is a color variation of the famous Royal Coachman. I tie the body first. Wind on several turns of peacock herl to form the rear butt section. Now tie in yellow floss and wrap evenly from rear butt up ⅔ of hook shank. I often give it a double layer of floss. Tie off floss and tie in another peacock herl. Form forward butt in the same manner as the rear butt. White goose primary flight feathers can be used in place of white duck.

87 **COACHMAN, LEAD WING** I prefer a Mustad hook #9671. If dark brown (coachman brown) hen hackle is not available, use softest coachman brown cock hackle. The wings can be either dark gray duck or goose quill sections.

87 **COACHMAN, ROYAL** I use a Mustad hook, #9671 or #9672. Tie the body first, then wind on several turns of peacock herl to form rear butt section. Tie in red floss and wrap evenly from rear butt up ⅔ of hook shank, using a double layer of floss. Tie off floss and tie in a second peacock herl. Form forward butt in same manner as rear. White goose primary flight feathers can be used in place of white duck.

87 **COWDUNG** I prefer a Mustad #9671 hook. The body can be made from either wool or floss. Wing quills can be either goose or duck dyed darkest brown. If brown hen hackle is not readily available, use softest cock hackle.

87 **DARK STONE FLY** I use a Mustad #9672 hook for this fly. The tail is dyed from dark brown turkey tail (short), and the body is ribbed with heavy gray sewing thread. After finishing off head of this fly, a dot of orange lacquer is placed directly on top of the head.

87 **EARLY BROWN STONE (Jennings)** I use a Mustad hook, #9671 for this fly. The wing is tied with two rusty dun hackle points. Take great care in placing these hackle points flat, directly on top of the body. **ART**
87 **FLICK'S VARIATION:** Art's pattern calls for no tail, and in place of dubbing seal fur, he uses stripped hackle stem from a reddish brown cock neck. The rest of the pattern is the same as Jennings'. The hackle stem should be well soaked in water before it's wound.

87 **GINGER QUILL** I prefer to use a Mustad hook #9671 or #7957BX. The tail should be several fibers from a medium ginger hackle. The body is stripped peacock quill (soaked well before using). Hackle

can be either ginger hen or softest medium cock hackle. The wings can be tied from either gray duck or gray goose primary flight feathers.

87 **GOLDEN STONE** I recommend a Mustad hook #9672 for this fly. For the tail I dye a mottled turkey wing quill gold and use several fibers of this tied in short. The body is ribbed with a heavy gold sewing thread. After ribbing, tie in a collar of soft hackle dyed gold and then tie in a small throat of teal flank dyed gold.

87 **THE GRANNOM** I recommend a Mustad hook #9671 or #9672. The tail for this fly is dyed olive hackle feathers. If you wish, the tail can be completely omitted from the pattern. The body can be either dark brown wool or floss.

87 **GRAY HACKLE** I recommend a Mustad hook #7957BX or #9671. After tying in the tail of red wool, separate wool fibers with your dubbing needle. The peacock herl body can be wound on conventionally or using the rope twist method I mentioned for the Zug Bug Nymph. The collar should be the softest grizzly hackle available.

87 **GREENWELL'S GLORY** I recommend using a Mustad #9671 or #9672 hook. For this fly I prefer to use light ginger hen hackle. However, the old English pattern refers to a hackle they call Greenwell. This is nothing more than a light furnace. An English substitute for this feather is to wind on a black ostrich herl and then wind your ginger hackle directly over the herl. When finished this gives the desired two-tone effect.

88 **GRIZZLY KING** I prefer to use a Mustad hook #9671 for this fly. For

the tail a section of dyed red goose or duck quill will do nicely. Ribbing should be fine flat gold tinsel evenly spaced up to the head. The hackle can either be grizzly hen or softest cock hackle available.

88 **GOLD RIBBED HARE'S EAR** The hook for this fly can either be Mustad #9671 or #7957BX. For dubbing I blend the longer hare's mask fur with the shorter ear fur. Ribbing can be the finest oval tinsel or fine flat gold tinsel. The legs are represented by simply picking out some of the body fur with a dubbing needle.

88 **HENDRICKSON, DARK** I recommend a Mustad hook #9671 for this fly. The tail can be either dyed dun hackle fibers or a few wood duck flank feathers or Mallard dyed wood duck color. Hackle can be either dyed dun hen or softest cock hackle.

88 **HENDRICKSON, LIGHT** I use a Mustad hook #9671. The tail can be either light dun hackle fibers or several fibers from a wood duck flank feather. The wing can be either natural wood duck flank or dyed from a Mallard. The original body calls for urine stained fox belly, but this is not readily available. For a substitute I blend either cream fox, or bleached raccoon with a pinch of pink rabbit. This will give you the necessary subtle pink cast.

88 **IRON BLUE DUN** I prefer a Mustad hook, either #9671 or #7957BX. Tie in several furnace hackle fibers for the tail. The tip is of red floss wound up one quarter of the hook shank. For the remainder of the body I use muskrat fur. Hackle can either be furnace hen hackle or mottled brown hen body feathers.

The wings can be either dark gray duck or goose primary flight feathers.

88 **LITTLE MARRYATT** I recommend a Mustad hook #9671 for this fly. For the body I blend medium yellow and golden tan rabbit fur. The wings are from the lightest gray secondary flight feathers found on the complete Mallard wing. The hackle can be either pale ginger hen or softest golden ginger cock hackle.

88 **McGINTY** I recommend a Mustad hook #7957BX or #9671 for this pattern. For the tail I tie in a few fibers of teal flank and over this a few fibers of dyed red cock hackle. When tying the body of this fly be sure to use the same size chenilles in black and yellow. Take one turn of black chenille and tie off. Tie in yellow chenille and take one turn directly in front of black. Again, tie off. Repeat this procedure alternating colors until you get to the head. Care should be taken in selecting chenille sizes as the body calls for only three bands of color. For the wing select two matching white tipped iridescent blue feathers from a complete pair of Mallard wings. Great care should be taken in matching these feathers.

88 **MARCH BROWN** I prefer a Mustad hook #9671 for this fly. I dub the body from sandy brown hare's mask fur. For the tails and legs of this fly, wood duck or grouse can be substituted for the brown partridge.

88 **MONTREAL** I use either a Mustad #9671 or #7957BX for this fly. The tail is a very narrow section of duck or goose quill dyed red. Take care to build a nicely tapered body while working with the floss.

88 **MORMON GIRL** I prefer a Mustad hook #9671 for this fly. The wing on this fly is made from a whole Mallard flank feather of medium size. Bunch the fibers of the tip together and tie them in as a bunch rather than cutting strips from each side of the stem. It's not a very well known fly, but can often come in handy when fishing murky water in early spring.

89 **ORANGE FISH HAWK** I use a Mustad hook #7957BX or #9671 for this pattern. When tying in the floss body, take care to keep body as thin and streamlined as possible. Both tag and rib are of fine flat gold tinsel. Badger hackle should be slightly soft cock hackle, wound on as a collar wet fly style, and stroked back as it is wound.

89 **PARMACHENE BELLE** I prefer a Mustad hook #9671 for this beautiful fly. The tail consists of red and white hackle fibers mixed and tied in together. The wing may seem like the most difficult to make on this fly, but by observing a few simple rules you can soon get the hang of it. To make the two "mixed" wings you should select two matching pairs of goose quill sections, one left and one right. These should be cut the same size as if you were making an ordinary wing for, let's say, a number 10 wet fly. Now cut two sections from the red wing quills in the same manner but only a third as wide as the white ones. Let's make the right wing first. Take the white wing quill section and split it lengthwise down the middle so that you have two sections the same size. Separate a narrow strip from the red quill section and then grasp one white strip by the butt and hold it between your thumb and first

finger—position the red strip directly underneath and line up the tip with the white section. Place the other white section under the red and stroke all three pieces together with your fingers. Do the same with the left wing and then tie both of them in together. This operation may not be successful the first time, but a little practice will ultimately give you the desired result. The hackle for this fly is wound from one red and one white cock hackle of wet fly quality.

PICKET PIN I recommend a Mustad hook #9672. Be sure to tie in the brown hackle before winding on the peacock herl body. Then spiral brown hackle over the body. Be careful to align tips of squirrel wing before tying in. Clip off wing butt closely. Form a head with peacock herl.

PINK LADY I use a Mustad hook #9671 for this fly. A light ginger cock hackle can be used in place of hen hackle. The wing should be tied from palest gray duck quill.

PROFESSOR I use a Mustad hook #9671 for this pattern. The tail of the fly is a very small section of dyed red Mallard wing. The wing is tied from a bunched section of Mallard duck flank.

QUILL GORDON I use a Mustad #7957BX hook for this pattern. Before tying this fly pre-soak your stripped peacock quills to prevent breaking during tying. Because peacock is such a fragile material it would be advisable to wrap fine gold wire counter-clockwise over the finished peacock body. The wire should be tied in before the body is applied.

RIO GRANDE KING I use a Mustad #9671 or #7957BX for this fly. Be careful to use a chenille of proportionate size to the size of the fly you are tying. For smaller flies, use finer chenille—and as the flies get larger, use proportionately larger chenille. The hackle can be either brown hen hackle or softest brown cock hackle.

WHITE MILLER I prefer a Mustad hook #9671 for this pattern. The tail and body are separately tied from the whitest cock or hen hackle available. Rib is of fine flat silver tinsel. This fly can be fished for smallmouth bass as well as trout.

WICKHAMS FANCY I recommend a Mustad hook #9671 for this fly. Before winding on the medium flat gold tinsel body, be sure to tie in the hackle for the rib. After the tinsel body is wound on, palmer the hackle forward to the head of the fly. Wings should be set between palmered hackle rib. Tie in the wing in the conventional wet fly manner.

YELLOW WOOLLY WORM I recommend a Mustad hook #9671 or #9672. Both partridge and furnace are acceptable variations in place of the grizzly hackle. Woolly worms can also be tied in brown, gray, black, green, olive, etc.

ZULU I prefer a Mustad hook #9671 or #9672 for this fly. I use long black saddle hackle. If not available, a long black cock hackle can be substituted. Prior to ribbing peacock herl body, tie in black hackle by the tip. When herl body is completed, palmer hackle in front of fly and tie off.

In palmering on wet flies, the proper procedure is to tie the hackle in by its tip, as opposed to the hackle butt section. This is done so that the hackle tapers from small at the rear to large at the head.

DRY FLIES

90 **ADAMS** The hook can be either a Mustad #94840 or #94833. For the body of this fly I prefer muskrat fur. The over-all hackle color is created by inter-winding a brown and a grizzly hackle. However, if you're lucky enough to own a well-marked dark cree neck, the hackles from this one neck alone will give you the same effect as the two hackles. An economical help would be to purchase the least expensive grizzly neck available, to be used solely where grizzly hackle tip wings are called for.

90 **ADAMS, SPENT WING** The hook can be either a Mustad #94840 or #94833. The Spent Wing Adams is like a regular Adams, but instead of the wings pointing upwards they are pulled down horizontally at right angles to the hook shank. They are then secured by using criss-cross windings between them.

90 **ANT, Black** I use a Mustad hook #94840 or #94833. When tying ants take care in defining the body shape. Both clumps should be very distinct. First tie in the rear clump of fur (this should be larger than the front). Then make one or two turns of stiff black hackle. Hackle on the ant should be kept as sparse as possible. Then tie in the front clump of dubbing and finish off. For the dubbing of this fly, I prefer to use either beaver or muskrat dyed black. However, dyed black rabbit can also be used.

90 **ANT, BLACK FLYING** I prefer a Mustad hook #94840 or #94833. This fly is exactly like the conventional black ant except for the wings. After tying in the rear body section, place two black hackle points directly on top, slanting back over the rear section. After tying in the wings, wind hackle over wing butts and finish this fly in the same manner as the conventional black ant.

90 **ANT, Red** I recommend a Mustad hook #94840 or #94833. On the smaller sizes I often use an up-eyed Mustad hook #94842. This fly is tied in the same manner as the conventional black ant, except that the colors of the materials are different. As an alternative to blue dun hackle for this fly, a medium ginger or cinnamon color hackle may be used. For the fur I use cream opossum or rabbit dyed cinnamon.

90 **BADGER SPIDER** For this fly I use a Mustad #9479 or #9523 hook. Most fly tyers make the mistake of selecting a hackle for spiders from the larger feathers at the top of the neck. Actually, the stiffest hackle comes off the side of the neck and is called spey hackle. A properly prepared neck skin should have these feathers on it. Select the longest and stiffest fibers for the tail of this fly. The body is wound from a stripped hackle stem, or if you wish, this fly can be tied with no body at all. Hackle is wound in the conventional manner and should be at least three times the width of the hook gap.

90 **BEAVERKILL, FEMALE** I use a Mustad hook #94840 or #94833. After tying in the tail, construct an egg sac of either yellow wool or fine yellow chenille. Take only one turn to form the egg sac. For the body I use muskrat. The wings are tied from two sections of natural gray duck quills.

BEAVERKILL, MALE For this fly I prefer either Mustad #94840 or #94833. This fly is tied in the same manner as the conventional dry fly except for the addition of a palmered body hackle. After tying in the tail, tie in the tip of a brown hackle and then finish floss underbody. After completing the body, spiral body hackle to front of fly and tie off.

BEETLE, Black For this fly I use either Mustad #94840 or #94833. In tying this fly I recommend either monocord or a strong black tying thread. Cut a section of deer body hair with the natural tips extending ¼ inch past the eye of the hook. Take several tight turns of thread to secure the hairs to the shank. Making sure the hair is secured, tightly wind the thread back to the bend and then back up to the original tie-in point. Now grasp the hairs that extend past the hook eye and pull back several on each side of the hook to form legs. Figure-eight the thread around the legs to secure them perpendicular to the body and take one or two turns directly in front of the legs. Clip off the hairs right behind the hook eye. Grasp the hair at the bend of the hook and pull it forward tightly over the body, then bind hair down with a few turns at a point half way between the eye of the hook and the legs. Now tie off at this point with a whip finish. Then grasp the rear of the body with your thumb and forefinger and roll the hair shell between your fingers to form a flatter silhouette. Clip the head to shape and lacquer the head and shell. Trim the legs to proper length. Your fly is now complete.

BEETLE, WOOD I recommend a Mustad hook #94840. Be sure to use heavy tying thread. Cut a section of deer body hair and tie in the natural tips lightly behind the eye of the hook. Roll the hair so it encircles the hook shank. Rib thread tightly back to the bend. At this point the hair should be securely attached to the shank. Wind the thread half way back towards the eye. Clip off the tips closely at the original tie-in point. Now, grasping the hair at the bend of the hook, pull forward around the body. Take several turns of thread around this hair at the midway point. From hair that extends past this tying point, pull back three hairs on each side of the shank (for legs). Take one or two turns (only) directly in front of the legs. Raise the remaining hair and wind the thread over under body to a point just behind the hook eye. Grasp the remaining hair and pull it forward over the hook eye. Then take a few turns of thread to secure the hair and tie off with a whip finish. Trim the head to shape. Separate the legs and lacquer the back of the fly.

BIRD'S STONE FLY I use a Mustad hook #79580. The tails and the antennae can either be moose body hair or fine peccary hair. After tying in the two tails, tie in a large furnace saddle or neck hackle. Now tie in the orange wool and wrap it up two-thirds of the hook shank. Spiral the furnace hackle-body and tie it off. The hackle is then clipped on top, bottom and sides. Take a bunch of natural brown bucktail and carefully align the tips then tie it directly over the body. Use care to clip excess butt as close to the body as possible. Now tie in two furnace hackles and wind them over the wing butts to the eye in conventional dry fly manner. Tie in two moose body hairs extending over the eye of the hook and whip finish off the head. Clip the front hackle flat on top and bottom.

BI-VISIBLE, Brown   I use a Mustad hook #94840 or #94833. After tying in the tail, tie in the long brown hackle by its tip. Proceed to palmer the hackle up the hook shank, taking turns as closely as possible and as far as the hackle will go. If necessary, tie in another brown hackle and palmer three-fourths up the hook shank. This brown hackle should graduate in size from smaller near the tail to larger near the front of the fly. Finally tie in one white hackle and make two or three turns. Tie off and whip finish.

BLACK GNAT   I prefer Mustad hook #94840 or #94833. I highly recommend the use of dyed black hackle for this fly. Natural black hackles are usually not of dry-fly quality. Also, the original pattern calls for a body of chenille. I often substitute dyed black beaver for better floatation.

BLUE DUN SPIDER   I use a Mustad hook #9479 or #9523 for this fly. Both tail and hackle of this fly should be the longest and stiffest available. Use the spey hackle on the sides of the neck skin. The body should be a stripped gray hackle stem or, if you wish, the body can be omitted.

BLUE QUILL   The hook can be either Mustad #94850 or #94833. Before tying this fly, the stripped peacock herl should be very well soaked in water. If not, it will break or crack when being wound on. The body can also be reinforced by a fine diameter gold wire wound in the opposite direction of the quill.

BLUE WINGED OLIVE   I use a hook #94840 or #94833. For the body fur, I blend medium olive rabbit and sulphur yellow rabbit fur. Wings are dark gray hackle points tied in the conventional dry-fly manner.

BLUE-WINGED OLIVE, Cut Wing   For this fly I use a Mustad hook #94842. This is an up-eyed hook for the reason that a down-eyed would be down in the surface film and distort the fly too much when seen from below the surface. Tie in the tail first in a conventional manner, then take a couple of turns of tying thread directly around the fibers close to the hook and raise them to a 45 degree angle. Hold them there and take a couple of turns around the hook shank close to the tie-in point and apply a drop of cement. This method will anchor the tails in a permanent position. The wings are cut to shape from a dark blue rooster or hen body feather, or one can use a very webby rooster or hen neck hackle. The important thing is to select feathers that are of the same size and have the same curvature and, needless to say, they should closely resemble the color wings you are trying to imitate—in this case, dark blue gray. Start by peeling the soft fibers of the butt section off the feathers and make sure that the fibers left on the stem are directly across from each other.

The lowest fibers will be the base of the wing. Measure the wing length from this point up the stem and cut away the surplus with a cross-cut, as if you were cutting the feather in half. Tie in the wings in the same manner as you would a pair of fan wings. The hackle is tied in directly in front of the wing and projecting forward over the hook eye with the best side up. Now take the thread to the rear of the fly and apply the dubbing, which is now wound forward closely to the wing. Lift the hackle out of the way and apply a couple of turns in front of the wing. Wind the hackle parachute style directly around the wing stems, taking each turn of hackle under the preceding one. Tie off in front and the fly is finished.

91 **BLUE-WING SULPHUR DUN (Thorax Tie)** For this fly I use a Mustad hook #94833. Start the fly by preparing the wings in the same manner as for the **Blue-Winged Olive, Cut Wing** and attach them in the middle of the shank. Fasten them in the same manner as fan wings and anchor the stems with thread along the shank. Now tie in the tails at the hook bend. They should be splayed and can be raised a little by taking some thread windings around the shank behind and pulling each turn in close to the base of the tails. Dub some fur on the thread and wind it up to the wing. This fur will act as a base for the hackle. Now tie in the two hackles together in front of the wing with the tips projecting toward the rear. Vincent C. Marinaro, the distinguished American angler and author who designed the thorax style dry flies, recommends using one

hackle with fibers a little shorter than the other. Grasp the long-fibered hackle and take a couple of windings on top in front of the wing and the windings behind the wing underneath the shank. Tie off the hackle closely in front of the wing and trim the surplus. Now grasp the short-fibered hackle and take several turns in a clockwise direction, laying the turns on top of the hook behind the wing and in front of the wing underneath. In this manner the hackle is applied in an "X" design. It should also be pointed out that the fly will now lean forward on the shorter fibers in front for better balance. Now fill in the space in front between the wing and the eye with fur and tie off.

91 **BROWN HACKLE** I use a Mustad hook #94840 or #94833. I use fine flat gold tinsel and take several turns at the bend of the hook to formulate the rear tag. The remainder of this fly is tied in the conventional dry fly manner.

91 **BUCKTAIL CADDIS** For this fly I use a heavy wire Mustad hook #3906B or #9672. Tie in a long brown saddle or neck hackle by the tip. Wind on the wool to just behind the eye of the hook and spiral the hackle up to and over the body, taking one or two extra turns at this point. Tie in a wing of natural brown bucktail so that it slants back over the body. Clip the wing butts closely and finish the head in the normal manner.

91 **CADDIS, DELTA WING, Ginger** My preference for this fly is a Mustad hook #94840 or #94833. This fly has no tail. For the dubbing of this fly I blend light ginger mink and

medium olive rabbit fur. Select two matched ginger hackle points. Strip to proper length and tie them in one at a time. When properly tied in, the hackle tips should be parallel to the sides of the fly and lay perfectly flat. Great care should be taken when setting these wings. When positioned properly, secure them with a drop of cement. Wind on one or two hackles in conventional dry fly manner and finish off the head.

92 CADDIS, HAIR WING, Gray For this fly I use a Mustad #94840 or #94833 hook. For the body of this fly I either use muskrat fur or gray mink tail underfur. I make the wing from mink tail guardhairs. Wind the body fur on ⅔ of the hook shank. Now cut a large bunch of mink tail guardhairs and carefully align the tips before tying them directly on top of the hook shank. After you have secured the wing with two or three turns of thread, roll the wing so that it comes down slightly on each side of the fly. Trim the butts at an angle as closely as possible. I prefer to securely lock the wing with a few drops of Plio-Head Cement, but a few drops of head lacquer placed on the wing butts will also do nicely. The hackle is then wound in the conventional dry fly manner. Since there are more than 2000 caddis species, colors vary tremendously, and these instructions will serve for them all. However, the most common are gray, brown, olive and tan.

92 CAENIS SPINNER, FEMALE I recommend a Mustad hook #94840 or #94832 for this fly. The tail should be three very pale blue dun hackle fibers spread widely. The abdomen can be either one white moose mane hair wound on, or white dubbing fur. If you use fur, dub it very thinly. After tying off the abdomen, take a piece of white Polypropylene yarn and lay it across the hook shank at the wing position, then secure it with several figure eight turns around the wing and hook shank. A drop of lacquer at this point will set the wings permanently. The thorax is dubbed from black rabbit or natural black mink fur. Wrap the thorax area with dubbing in a figure eight, encompassing the wing tie-in area at the same time. The finished thorax should appear thickly dubbed. Trim the wing length to shape.

The male Caenis Spinner is exactly the same as the female except the body is all black. Again, take care in keeping the abdomen very, very thin.

92 CAHILL, DARK I recommend a Mustad hook #94840 or #94833 for this fly. I dub the body of this fly from gray muskrat fur. For the wings I prefer to use natural wood duck flank, but dyed Mallard flank will also do nicely.

92 CAHILL, LIGHT I use a Mustad hook #94840 or #94833 for this fly. For the tail of this fly I prefer to use the longest and stiffest light ginger hackle fibers I have. The traditional pattern calls for a tail of wood duck flank fibers but I do not think they float the fly as well as hackle fibers. For the body of this fly any light cream fur will do. Bleached Australian opossum, bleached raccoon, or even kapok will do nicely.

92 COACHMAN For this fly I use a Mustad hook #94840. The wings of this fly can either be white duck or white goose primary wing quills.

After tying in the wing, durability can be increased by giving the inner sides of both wings a thin coat of vinyl cement. They will now last many times longer than the traditionally frail upright quill wings.

92 COACHMAN, FAN-WING, ROYAL
For this fly I recommend a Mustad hook #94840. Make sure markings of golden pheasant tippet fibers are aligned when tying in the tail. After tying in the butt of a peacock herl, tie off and tie in one or two strands of red floss. After double wrapping the middle section with red floss, tie it off and tie in another peacock herl. Wrap on the front butt section. An alternative method for doing the body: after tying off the rear butt of peacock herl, pull the remainder forward and tie it down at the front butt area. Now tie in the red floss and complete the floss section. Then use the remaining peacock herl to form the front butt. This not only saves herl but much valuable time. The wings of this fly are best tied from the white breast feathers of a wood duck. The feathers should be matched in size and curve. Strip off lower fibers to desired wing length and hold the wings together while tying in the stems as you would hackle point wings. However, once tied in, do not let go, but pull them back along the hookshank and take several turns of thread, binding them down on the shank. If the feathers are released before this step, they will almost always twist. The hackle is then wound in conventional dry fly manner.

92 COACHMAN, LEAD WING I use a Mustad hook #94840. This fly is exactly like the standard Coachman dry fly except that instead of using white goose or duck primary quills, I use a natural gray primary quill from a Mallard duck.

92 COACHMAN, ROYAL I prefer a Mustad hook #94840. The body of this fly is exactly the same as the Fan Wing Royal Coachman. In fact, the only difference is that the wing is tied from a section of white goose or duck primary quills.

93 COACHMAN, ROYAL PARACHUTE
I use a Mustad #94840. Select a bunch of white calftail and tie it in at the wing position with the tips extending forward over the eye of the hook. After securing the butt firmly, raise the wing and take several turns of thread in front of it. Now take several turns around the base of the wing to lock it in upright position. Wind the thread back to the tail and secure the wing with a drop of Plio-Head Cement. The body is now tied exactly like the body of the Royal Coachman. After completing the body, tie in one or two hackles and wind them around the wing base in parachute fashion.

93 CRANE FLY SKATER For this fly I use a Mustad hook #9523, but any short shank up-eye hook will do. This fly consists of two feathers only—one for the body and wings, and one for the hackle (legs). The fly was designed by Harry Darbee, a distinguished American angler and fly dresser who has many other fine flies on the list of famed patterns. Select a Mallard side feather large enough for the size fly you are tying. Hold it by the tip and stroke the fibers in reverse down toward the base. Crowd the fibers close to the feather stem and tie it in on the hook about ⅛ inch from the eye with the tip portion and the crowded fiber bunch projecting toward the rear. The free fibers extending to each side in front are now fashioned into two large spent wings. Secure the feather very tightly on the shank so it does not turn. I often apply a little cement to fix the structure firmly. The crowded bunch of fibers are now fashioned into the body by applying cement or rubber glue. When it's well formed you can trim away the tip portion. Attach the hackle and wind it parachute style around the tie-in position: that is, between the body extension and the hook shank in the rear and in front on top of the hook. Tie it off and apply some cement where the hackle stem goes around the body.

93 **CREAM VARIANT**   For this fly I use a Mustad hook #94838. The tail should be the longest and stiffest cream hackle fibers available. The body is wound from a stripped cream hackle stem. Soak this hackle stem well in water before using or it will split while being wound. For the hackle of this fly select a spey hackle off the edge of the neck skin. This hackle is usually longer and stiffer than the larger hackles at the top of the neck. Wind the hackle in conventional dry fly manner.

93 **DUN VARIANT**   I use a Mustad hook #94838. The tail for this fly should be the longest and stiffest hackle fibers available. For the body I use a stripped brown hackle stem, well soaked in water before using. After completing the body I lacquer it to protect it and also to bring out the color definition. The hackle on this fly should be the longest and stiffest available. Use the spey hackle found on the edge of the neck skin.

93 **EPHORON SPINNER**   For this pattern I use a Mustad hook #94840 or #94833. The body of this fly is made from a white porcupine bristle. Do not mistake this for the thick pointed quills of porcupine fame. The bristle I talk about is longer and thinner than the quills and much more flexible. Be sure to select the lightest of these fibers and use only the light base section. Take a piece of Polypropylene yarn and lay it across the hook shank and tie it in with figure eight turns of thread and secure with a drop of head lacquer. For the thorax I dub white rabbit on the thread and overlap the wing tie-in area with figure eight turns of dubbing. Tie off behind the hook eye.

93 **FURNACE SPIDER**   I use a Mustad hook #9479 or #9523. The tail should be the longest and stiffest furnace hackle fibers available. After winding on the body I lacquer it to protect it and bring out the color definition. Select the longest and stiffest spey hackle from the edge of a furnace neck skin and take three or four turns in conventional dry fly style.

93 **GINGER QUILL**   I use Mustad hook #94840 or #94833. The body of this fly is stripped peacock herl from the eye section of the tail feathers. The light to dark markings are more defined in this area of the peacock tail. Be sure to soak this quill well before using or it will crack while being wound. After completing the body I lacquer it to protect it and increase its durability.

93 **GREEN DRAKE, Cut Wing (Poul's)** I use a Mustad hook #94842. This fly is tied in the exact same manner as the **Blue-Wing Olive, Cut Wing**

and only the coloration and type of material is different.

93 **GREEN DRAKE SPINNER (Coffin Fly)** For this fly I use a Mustad hook #94838. The body of this fly is the white end of a porcupine quill. Cut the quill to length (approximately ⅞ inch) and remove the pith from the inside with your dubbing needle. Now push the needle through and penetrate the tip completely. Select three moose mane fibers and insert them in the quill. Guide them through the hole in the tip portion and extend them beyond the tip for the proper tail length, or approximately one body length. Apply a little cement on the tip of the quill and the tail fibers to secure them. Now tie the extension on the hook very securely, and at the same time secure the butt ends of the tail fibers. Select the hackle with fibers long enough to be fashioned into wings of the proper length. Wind the hackle on the shank fairly heavy and wide. When it is wound on, tie it off and trim the hackle flat on the top and bottom for a spent-wing effect.

93 **GRAY FOX (Flick)** I use a Mustad hook #94840 or #94833 for this fly. It is simpler to use light fawn fox if you have it, but the ultimate color that you could use is a golden tannish ginger. If you don't have the necessary fox, a similar shade can be blended from dyed rabbit.

94 **GRAY-FOX VARIANT** For this pattern I use a Mustad hook #94838. The tail should be the longest and stiffest medium ginger hackle fibers, but bleached medium ginger mink tail guardhairs are also ideally suited for the tails. The body is a stripped cream hackle stem well soaked in water before using. For the hackle I use one medium ginger, one light ginger, and one grizzly hackle interwound separately. Be careful to match evenly the size of all three hackles.

94 **HENDRICKSON, DARK** I use a Mustad hook #94840 or #94833 for this fly. The tail can either be several wood duck flank fibers or stiff dun hackle fibers, which float the fly better than wood duck flank. The body of this fly is ideally made from well blended red fox back, which gives you a dark reddish gray color dubbing. If this is not available, dark muskrat fur may be substituted.

94 **HENDRICKSON DUN, THORAX** I use a Mustad hook #94833. For the body I use a combination of natural tan raccoon and dyed pink rabbit. Except for the different colors in the materials used this fly is tied in the same manner as the **Blue-Wing Sulphur Dun, Thorax.**

94 **HENDRICKSON, FEMALE** I prefer a Mustad hook #94840 or #94833 for this fly. The tail is traditionally tied from medium blue dun hackle fibers but I now prefer medium gray mink tail guard hairs. The body calls for pink vixen fox fur, but this is rather hard to come by. An ideal substitute is to use cream gray fox belly and pink rabbit, well blended.

94 **HENDRICKSON, LIGHT** I use a Mustad hook #94840 or #94833. The tail of this fly can either be several wood duck flank fibers or medium blue dun hackle fibers. The body is tied from cream fox belly, but if you prefer, a pinkish cast can be added by blending belly fur with a touch of dyed pink rabbit.

94 **HENDRICKSON, SPINNER** For this pattern I use a Mustad hook #94840 or #94833. The wings for this fly are from a conventionally tied dry fly hackle. Start by winding the hackle on in a normal dry fly manner, then divide the hackle fibers into two equal bunches, one on each side of the hook shank. Figure eight between them and then take one or two turns of tying thread around their base close to the hook. Add a drop of head cement on the windings. Wind the thread back to the rear of the hook and tie in three or four hackle fibers for the tail. The body is now dubbed and wound up to the wings and figure eight between them. Take a few turns of fur in front of the wing and tie off. For the blend of this body I use a deep reddish brown dyed rabbit or dyed mink.

94 **HENRYVILLE SPECIAL** I use a Mustad hook #94840 or #94833. Wind the thread to the bend of the hook. Tie in the body material which can be olive floss or fluorescent green floss. At this time also tie in the tip of a grizzly hackle. Wind the floss ⅔ up the hook shank. Tie it off and palmer the grizzly hackle up to tie-off position. Tie in a few strands of wood duck flank feather directly on top of the shank. At this point take two sections of gray duck wing quill and tie them in wet fly fashion over the wood duck underwing. The finished wing should be tent shaped. Now tie in a brown hackle in conventional dry fly style.

94 **HOOPER, JOE'S** I use a Mustad hook #9672. First prepare the wing quills. Select two matching mottled brown turkey wing feathers and cut a matched section from each quill.

Now apply some vinyl cement on each quill section and set aside to dry. The tail is a large bunch of red hackle fibers tied slightly down on the hook bend to get a downward slant. Tie in a brown saddle hackle or large brown cock hackle at the tail. Tie in the chenille and form a loop that extends over the tail. Tie off the chenille at the hook bend. Wrap the remainder of the chenille ⅔ up the hook shank and tie off. Now palmer the saddle hackle up the entire length of the body and tie it off. Now trim the hackle on all sides of the fly. Tie in the prepared wing sections with the dull side facing outwards. First secure the farthest wing on the side of the fly body, then tie in the wing on the near side. Tie down the wing butts and trim surplus closely, then tie in one brown and one grizzly hackle and wind them in conventional dry fly style.

94 **HOPPER, WHITLOCK'S** I recommend a Mustad hook #79580 for this fly. It's best to prepare the wing feather first so it can dry well before it's tied in. Spray a well mottled turkey wing quill with Krylon. When it is dry, cut a quill section ⅜ to ½ inch wide, depending on the size fly you are tying. Trim away the tip portion and round the end of the section to be used. Now tie in the red deer body hair at the bend so it slants down a little. The extended butt ends are tied down on top of the shank and will act as an underbody. Make sure to leave ⅓ of a hook length distance between the eye and the beginning of the body. Tie in the brown hackle at the bend together with the wool. Now form a loop with the wool so it extends to the rear over the tail, then tie it

down at the tie-in position. Wind the tying thread forward, binding the short wool end down on top of the shank in the process. Wind the body and palmer the brown hackle. Now tie in the yellow deer hair underwing securely and lay the turkey overwing flat on top. Secure it with several turns of thread and apply some cement. Tie in the natural deer body hair in front so the tips reach halfway down the wing. Tie in some additional bunches of deer hair and tie off. The head is now trimmed to shape, leaving only some long hair tips as a collar. Work a few drops of Plio-Head Cement into the fly head to secure the spun hair.

HUMPY I use a Mustad hook #94840 or #3906. Tie in a section of deer body hair for the tail. After securing it firmly, tie in another section of deer body hair by the butts, making sure the hair is long enough to form both the body and the wings of the fly. After securing the butts right behind the wing position the thread should be wound back to the hook bend, binding the hair down to form an underbody. Now wind the thread back to the wing position, making sure that the thread completely covers hair and hook shank. The color of the thread you use will be the body color of the finished fly. Pull the extending deer hair tips forward over the underbody and the eye of the hook and secure body with several turns of thread. Take the hair tips extending over eye and pull them back to an upright position. Take a few turns in front of wings to secure them in an upright position. Divide the hair tips into two wings and figure eight with the tying thread. Tie in the

hackle in conventional dry fly manner.

HUMPY, ROYAL This fly is tied exactly as the Humpy above, only the material list is different.

INCH WORM I use a Mustad hook #94840 or #94833. Take a bunch of long dyed green deer body hair approximately one-half the diameter of the finished body. Lay deer hairs over the hook shank with the hook eye under the middle point of the hairs. Secure hairs behind the hook eye and, rolling the hairs around the hook shank, wrap tightly back to the bend of the hook. Wind the thread back to approximately where the head segment of the worm should be. Now grasp the hairs extending past the eye of the hook and pull them backwards, making sure that they evenly surround the underbody. Holding all the hairs back tightly, take several turns of tying thread and whip finish off. Cut off thread and tie thread on, around body, to form another segment of equal size to the head segment. Whip finish and cut off the thread. Repeat this procedure for segmentation all the way down the hook shank and up the body extension. When proper body length is achieved, clip off remaining excess of tail of fly.

IRRESISTIBLE I use a Mustad hook #94840 for this pattern. Natural brown calftail or woodchuck guardhairs may be substituted in tying the wing and tail of this fly.

Tie in the tail and body first, then tie in the wing and hackle.

ISONYCHIA, CUT WING (Poul's) For this fly I use a Mustad hook #94842. I prefer to make the wing of either a natural dun hen body or neck feather, or the webby section of a dun rooster hackle. The wing itself is cut and trimmed to form the natural shape of a mayfly wing. The hackle is tied in parachute style on top of the hook shank, directly around the stems at the wing base. The tail extends upwards at a 45° angle. (See **Blue-Winged Olive, Cut Wing**.)

JASSID I use a Mustad hook #94840 for this pattern. A jungle cock tail is used to form the wing, but a ring neck pheasant or drake Mallard neck feather may be cut and lacquered as a substitute. The wing is tied flat on top of the hook shank to form an oval silhouette.

KING'S RIVER CADDIS For this pattern I use a Mustad hook #94840. The wing is a mottled turkey quill section tied tent-shaped and trimmed at a slight angle. I sometimes apply some Krylon on the quill section to prevent splitting.

LEAF ROLLER I use a Mustad hook #94840 for this fly. The body portion is cut from the butt-end of a mallard wing quill. The length depends on the size fly you are tying, but a good average is about one inch. To attach the hook I make a small hole in the quill at a point equal to the hook length measuring from the front of the quill section. Now apply some duco cement inside of the quill with your dubbing needle and insert the hook eye into the hole. Push the hook forward till the eye appears in front. Now fill in the hole in front with a small piece of cork or plastic cement. Color the whole body with a yellow-green waterproof marking pen and then give it at least two coats of clear nail polish.

LETORT CRICKET For this fly I use Mustad hook #94840. The wing is made from a section of dyed black goose or natural crow wing quill sprayed with Krylon and doubled lengthwise. The wing section itself is trimmed and rounded at the end. When tied in it slightly surrounds the body on each side. Black deer hair is then tied in to form a hair wing over the black underwing. The clipped head is formed by spinning and trimming the butt-ends of the black deer hair.

LETORT HOOPER I use a Mustad hook #94840 for this fly. It's tied in the exact same manner as the Letort Cricket except for the color of the materials.

MARCH BROWN A Mustad hook #94840 or #94833 is my preference. Since this is one of the larger Mayflies, the tail is extremely important. For this reason I now use bleached ginger mink tail guardhairs as they are much stiffer than the stiffest hackle. If fawn fox is not available I use tannish brown bleached Australian opossum for the body.

MARCH BROWN, REALISTIC (Poul's) For this fly I use a Mustad hook #94842. The best feather I have found for the tails and the extension on this fly is the ginger colored breast feather from a ring neck pheasant. It is the one with a distinct black mark at the tip. To prepare it I hold it by the tip and pull off all the fuzz and dark fibers on both sides of the stem. The remaining portion of the feather is now about one and one half inches long. Hold it again by the tip and draw the fibers on the lower one-half inch portion of the stem in reverse. Hold them in reversed position between your thumb and first finger, then apply some thick cement on the fibers. (Do not get cement on the tip portion.) Now draw the fibers between your fingers and compress them closely to the stem. The body is now formed. Separate one fiber on each side of the tip portion and cut away the section in between them. The two fibers represent the tails and can be reinforced by adding a drop of cement at their base. The extension is now cut to length, which is equal to the distance between the hook eye and the point of the hook plus 1/16 inch used for securing it on the hook. It's now tied in directly above the hook point with thread windings and some cement. (It must be secured very, very tightly.) The wing length for this fly is equal to the distance between the hook eye and the tip of the extension. The rest of the fly, that is the fur, tying in of the wings and winding of the hackle, is exactly the same as in the **Blue Wing Olive, Cut Wing.**

96 **MICHIGAN MAYFLY, REALISTIC (Poul's)** I prefer a Mustad hook #94842. Except for the difference in materials and final fly coloration, the tying instructions for this fly are exactly the same as for the **March Brown, Realistic.**

96 **MIDGE, ADAMS** I prefer a Mustad hook #94840 for this fly. This fly is identical to the standard Adams dry fly except that the grizzly hackle point wings are omitted.

96 **MIDGE, BLACK** I use a Mustad hook #94840 or #94842. Select the narrowest black ostrich herl for this fly. Black dubbing will also do nicely. For the hackle I prefer dyed black as the quality is usually superior to that of natural black hackle.

96 **MIDGE, BLACK HERL** I use a Mustad hook #94840 or #94842. The tail on this fly is optional. It is imperative to select the finest ostrich herl you can obtain. Otherwise the body will be over-sized for the hook. Herl midges may also be tied in any color you wish.

96 **MIDGE, NO NAME** I prefer a Mustad hook #94840 or #94842. The tail on this fly is optional. Since it does not take much to float it, try to keep the hackle sparse.

There are many different colors of natural midges, so you tie them in the colors of those found in the rivers you fish.

96 **MOSQUITO** I prefer a Mustad hook #94840 or #94833. Take great care in selecting one very light and one very dark moose mane hair. After tying them in, wind both hairs simultaneously to form the body. Make sure you have a smooth and tapered underbody before you start this procedure.

96 **MOUSE, DEER HAIR** I prefer a Mustad hook #9672. This pattern is highly recommended in Charlie Brooks' fine book *The Trout and the Stream*. Although a Western pattern, it makes a great night fly in the East. The tail should be a thin strip of chamois leather. If none is available, a rubber band will do. After spinning the deer hair, trim the body to an elongated tear drop shape. The bottom of the body should be trimmed flat, as close to the hook shank as possible. Use plenty of cement after spinning on each bunch of deer hair.

96 **NO HACKLE, SLATE TAN** I recommend a Mustad hook #94833. This fly represents a freshly emerged dun. The spreading of the tail is extremely critical on all no-hackle flies. Since there is no hackle for support, the tail must act as outriggers. Spin on a very small amount of dubbing at the bend to form a small ball. A good trick in tying this tail on is to tie the tail directly on top of the shank (normal style) and as you wind the thread back towards the dubbed ball, spread an equal amount of fibers on each side of the ball. As you approach the fur ball the thread pressure will cause the tail to flare widely. The wings of this fly are tied in wet fly fashion except that the natural curve is outwards. Take care when tying in the wings that they are on the sides of the body, not directly on top. Both wings should be tied in simultaneously.

96 **PALE EVENING DUN** I use a Mustad hook #94840 or #94833. The body fur should be dyed a very pale sulphur yellow. On some streams you might find the slightest touch of olive more closely represents the natural.

97 **PALE WATERY DUN** I use a Mustad hook #94840 or #94833 for this pattern. The body of this fly should be the palest yellow possible and is usually dyed rabbit. The wings are hackle tips from the palest blue dun. This very, very pale shade is often referred to as watery dun.

97 **POTAMANTHUS, CUT WING (Poul's)** For this fly I use a Mustad hook #94842. Except for the difference in color, the tying procedure is exactly the same as the **Blue-Wing Olive, Cut Wing.**

97 **POTAMANTHUS SPINNER** I use a Mustad hook #94840 or #94833 for this fly. The wing is tied in the same manner as that of the Hendrickson Spinner. Or, if you wish, gray Polypropylene yarn may be used. Instructions for the Potamanthus wing are given under **Ephoron Spinner.** The body of this fly should be a very pale yellow.

97 **QUILL GORDON** Use a Mustad hook #94840 or #94833. The body is tied in the exact same manner as the Blue Quill. I sometimes dye the stripped quill a very pale yellow to more closely match the natural insect. If available, I use a rusty medium blue dun hackle.

97 **RED QUILL** I use a Mustad hook #94840 or #94833. The body is tied from a stripped reddish brown cock hackle. It should be well soaked in water before it's wound on to prevent breaking. After the body is complete, give the quill a coat of clear lacquer to protect it and also to bring out the color definition.

97 **RENEGADE** I use a Mustad hook #94840. This fly is of the "Fore and Aft" design and is a famous and very productive western pattern. The two hackles serve well to float this fly in the turbulent western waters. Tie in a tag of fine flat gold tinsel going slightly down the bend. Tie in and wind a brown hackle immediately in front in the standard dry fly style. The middle section is peacock herl, and the front hackle is tied conventionally from white hackle.

97 **RIO GRANDE KING** I use a Mustad hook #94840. Although pattern calls for black chenille, wide black ostrich herl makes a body of superior floating ability.

97 **SOFA PILLOW, GRAY** For this pattern, I use a Mustad hook #9672. The tail is a section cut from a dyed yellow duck or goose primary feather. Tie the tail in on edge, directly on top of the hook shank. Be careful when tying in the wing to evenly align the tips of the squirrel hair. The finished wing should be the same length as the tail. A variation of this fly is the Brown Sofa Pillow. It calls for a red feather tail, red or orange floss body, a fox squirrel wing and a brown hackle.

97 **SPRUCE FLY** I recommend a Mustad hook #94840 or #3906 for this fly. If moose body hair is not available for the tail, I use natural black mink tail guardhairs. The rear of the body is tied from red floss; the front half of peacock herl.

97 **SULPHUR DUN, CUT WING (Poul's)** I use a Mustad hook #94842. The body is a strong sulphur yellow, which I dye from rabbit. Also, on many streams this fly has a definite orange tint. Tying instructions for this fly are the same as those given for the **Blue-Wing Olive Dun, Cut Wing.**

98 **SULPHUR DUN, LITTLE** I recommend a Mustad hook #94840 or #94833. The body should be a medium sulphur yellow. The hackle should be a very pale ginger, but not a light ginger. Wings are medium pale dun hackle tips.

98 **SULPHUR SPINNER** I use a Mustad hook #94840 or #94833. Except for color variations this fly is tied in exactly the same manner as the Hendrickson Spinner. A variation for the wings would be to use pale gray Polypropylene yarn. Tying in-

structions are given under **Ephoron Spinner.** Polypropylene wings are not only better for floatation, but greatly increase the angler's visibility of the fly.

98 **WULFF, BLONDE** I use a Mustad hook #94840 or #3906. If tan elk hair is not available, an interesting substitute is bleached ginger mink guardhairs. These hairs can be used for both the tail and the divided wings. For the body I use bleached Australian opossum.

98 **WULFF, GRAY** I use a Mustad hook #94840 or #3906 for this fly. The wings and tail for this fly can either be natural brown bucktail or natural or dyed brown calftail. I prefer to use medium gray muskrat fur for the body.

98 **WULFF, GRIZZLY** I use a Mustad hook #94840 or #3906 for this fly. The tail and wings can either be natural brown bucktail or natural or dyed brown calftail. Although the pattern traditionally calls for lacquered yellow floss body, I prefer to use bright yellow dubbing for added floatation.

98 **WULFF, ROYAL** I use a Mustad hook #94840 or #3906. The tail can be either natural brown or natural white bucktail. Or, if you wish, calftail may be used. The choice of color is up to you. The body is tied in the exact manner as given for the **Royal Coachman.** The wings can either be white bucktail or white calftail. Calftail is much easier to use.

98 **WULFF, WHITE** I recommend a Mustad hook #94840 or #3906. The tail and wings can either be natural white bucktail or natural white calftail. For the body I use white

mink body fur. The hackle should be the whitest badger available. If you do not have badger hackle, a pure white hackle of dry fly quality may be substituted.

STREAMERS

98 **ALASKA MARY ANN**   Use a Mustad hook #79580. If polar bear hair is not available, use imitation polar bear found at most shops or very long translucent hairs at the end of a natural white calftail. The natural curl of this calftail can be rolled out between your fingers.

98 **A. S. TRUDE**   I use a Mustad hook #79580. The body of this fly is wrapped with fine or medium oval tinsel. After tying the wing, a soft brown wet fly hackle should be tied on as a collar in traditional wet-fly fashion.

98 **BADGER STREAMER** A Mustad hook #79580 is used for this fly. The tail and cheeks of this fly are from a barred wood duck flank feather. After tying in the white bucktail underwing (shorter than tail) tie in four white badger hackles over the bucktail. Turn the fly back to upright position and tie in the strips of wood duck for the cheeks. Finish the head.

99 **BLACK GHOST** I use a Mustad hook #9575 for this fly but a #3665A hook may also be used. The wing of this fly is four long white saddle or cock neck hackles. A very deadly variation of this fly is the Marabou Black Ghost. Instead of tying the wing from hackles, tie in a sparse underwing of white bucktail. Over this tie a section of white marabou. The action of the marabou greatly enhances this already proven pattern.

99 **BLACK MARABOU**   The hook used for this fly is a Mustad #79580. Although the body calls for black wool or floss, many tyers prefer to use mylar piping. For this, first build up a wool underbody and then, after removing the threads from the center of the mylar piping, cut to proper length and slide piping over the hook eye and body. Using bright red thread, tie down the piping at the bend and whip finish. Tie down the piping at the wing position with black thread and proceed with pattern in the normal manner.

99 **BLACK NOSE DACE** I use a Mustad hook #79580 for this fly. Great care should be taken in keeping the wing in three distinct color layers and also in keeping the wing sparsely tied. For the body of this fly tie in medium oval silver tinsel at the tail and, after wrapping the body from medium flat silver tinsel, rib up to the wing position with the oval tinsel.

99 **BLACK NOSE DACE (Thunder Creek)**   For this fly I use a Mustad hook #36620. Start the fly by tying in the embossed silver tinsel $3/16$ inch from the hook eye and wind it back to the bend, then forward to the tie-in spot and tie it off. Take your tying thread back to the position that is a shade more than a hook gap distance from the eye. At this point tie in a sparse bunch of black bucktail with the tips extending one hook gap beyond the bend of the hook. Trim the butt ends to a taper and wind the tying thread around them to form a long narrow underhead. (This underhead should be a shade longer than the hook gap.) The length of the brown and white bucktail bunches we are now going

to tie in is very critical. Take a fairly long bunch of brown bucktail and even up the tips. Tie it in with a few turns of thread directly on top of the underhead and with the tips projecting forward over the eye. With some turns of thread over the bucktail as close to the eye as you can get, double back the bucktail to measure the length. It should project a little more than one hook gap beyond the bend. If not, loosen the thread windings and adjust the hair to the proper length. When the right length is obtained, secure the brown bucktail tightly and trim the butt ends on a slant a bit short of the length of the underhead. Turn the hook over in the vise and repeat the procedure with the white bucktail, securing it under the head. When both hair bunches are tied in, a smooth underhead is formed with tying thread. I sometimes apply some coats of cement for strength. Let the tying thread hang by the bobbin at a point where the underhead starts, then grasp the brown hair and pull it back over the underhead and body and take a couple of turns of threads around it. Now pull it very tight toward the rear and bind it down securely. Repeat the procedure with the white bucktail. At this point you must make sure that the hair at the head completely encircles the hook shank, and that the two colors are separate and distinctly defined. Now take several turns of red thread to complete the color band and whip finish. Give the head several coats of clear lacquer. When it is dry, paint a fine black lateral line on each side from the hook eye to the collar. The eyes are formed with a drop of yellow lacquer with a smaller drop of black lacquer for the pupil.

COCK-A-TOUCH   For this fly I use a Mustad hook #79580. For the tail, tie in several red hackle fibers short. Over this tie in two or three peacock herl tips and on each side of this two long badger hackles flaring outwards. Tie in the butt of peacock herl. Directly in front of this, tie in a collar of badger hackle in the traditional wet fly style. In front of this, tie in another peacock butt and then another badger hackle slightly larger than the first. Repeat this procedure two more times, taking care that each time the badger hackle is larger than the preceding hackle. The fly should be proportioned so that four peacock herl butts and four badger hackle collars completely cover the hook shank.

DARK SPRUCE   I use a Mustad hook #9672 for this fly. The tail is four or five peacock sword tips. The rear half of the body is red floss. The front half is heavily wrapped peacock herl. Over this is a wing of four dark furnace hackles and the collar is tied in wet fly style from a large soft furnace hackle.

DEER CREEK RAT   For this fly I use a Mustad hook #79580. The tail of this fly is five or six fibers from a cock pheasant center tail. The underwing is a small portion of natural brown bucktail. On each side of this underwing tie in one very dark brown hackle. The head is spun of black deer body hair (muddler minnow style), but clipped flat top and bottom. The sides are trimmed to a rounded arrow shape.

EDSON TIGER, DARK   I prefer a Mustad hook #9575 for this fly. The tail of this fly can be either yellow hackle tips or a bunch of yellow hackle fibers. The tail should be tied in directly on top of a small gold tag. The throat of this fly is tied very short from two dyed red hackle tips. You might find it easier to reverse the fly in the vise to tie in this throat.

99 **EDSON TIGER, LIGHT**   I use a Mustad hook #9575 or #3664A for this fly. The tail of this fly is a very narrow section from a barred wood duck flank feather tied in over a small gold tag. If this feather is not available, use natural guinea hen that has large white dots. A few fibers of this will do nicely. The body is completely of peacock herl, and I recommend using the long fine fibers at the base of a complete peacock eye. This will help to keep the body nice and slim. After the wing is tied in, a fine strip of red goose or a red hackle tip is tied in flat directly on top of the wing. Cheeks are of jungle cock and tied in very, very short.

99 **ESOPUS**   I use a Mustad hook #79580 for this fly. Be careful to keep the complete wing very sparse and colors well separated. The Esopus pattern is one of a series of flies developed on New York's Esopus Creek. Many combinations of colors can be used for the wing, usually with darker wings over the lighter underwing.

100 **FLOATING STREAMER**   This fly is highly recommended in Charles Brooks' book *The Trout and the Stream.* It adds an exciting new wrinkle to stream fishing for it is the ultimate combination of the streamer and the dry fly. Brooks recommends a perfect bend 8X long ring eye gold hook. If not available, use hook #36620. It is 6X long with a ring eye. Prepare a goose quill by cutting to proper length and removing all pith. Trim a cork cylinder or a piece of balsa wood into tapered shape to represent a minnow's head and also to act as the plug for the open quill end. Cement the cork into the end of the quill and also apply cement to the tapered tip end to insure the quill's water tightness. Wrap the hook shank from behind the eye to the bend and back with white tying thread as a base for the quill to set on. Where the quill joins the cork, lash down the quill directly on top of the hook shank with several turns of white tying thread. Take a long section of light green marabou and tie it down on top of the quill at this point. Spiral the thread back to the hook bend, making sure the marabou is directly on top of the quill and that the quill is directly on top of the hook shank. At the bend, take several turns of tying thread and then spiral back to the original tie-in point. Secure tightly with several turns and whip finish off. The eyes are formed with two drops of black lacquer on the cork head and after cementing the quill to the shank (over tie-in thread), put several red dots on the underbody and a larger red dot to represent the throat.

100 **GOLDEN DARTER**   I prefer a Mustad hook #9575 for this fly. The tail is a thin strip of mottled brown turkey wing. If not available, a section of pheasant or grouse wing will do nicely. The throat of this fly calls for a gray ginger cock body feather but, if not available, some hen neck shoulder feathers have a similar white strip down the center. This can be used in place of the jungle cock body feather. The feather should be tied flat under the wing body.

100 **GOLDEN SHINER (Thunder Creek)**   A Mustad hook #36620 should be used for this fly. The tying instructions are the same as given for the Black Nose Dace (Thunder Creek), except the body is embossed gold tinsel and the underwing is yellow bucktail. Also, no lateral stripe is painted on the head.

100 **GRAY GHOST** I use a Mustad hook #9575 for this fly. There has been much controversy over the wing color of this fly. Carrie Stevens' original pattern called for a medium gray saddle hackle with a definite olive cast. This was, however, to imitate the rock smelt bay fish. But, as this fly is now fished all over the country I honestly feel the ultimate wing color is not that critical. The shoulder of silver pheasant and cheek of jungle cock can be lacquered together in advance or tied in separately when needed. The body is of orange floss and great care should be taken to keep it as thin as possible. The red band on the head is optional, but the original pattern calls for it.

100 **GREEN COSSEBOOM** I prefer a Mustad hook #9672 for this fly. The tail is an extension of the light olive green floss used for the body. After tying in the wing, wind a collar of soft light greenish yellow hackle in the traditional wet-fly manner.

100 **GREEN GHOST** I use a Mustad hook #9575 for this pattern. This fly is identical to the Gray Ghost except that the wing is green instead of olive gray. The pattern was developed in an attempt to more closely resemble the smelt.

100 **HORNBERG** I use a Mustad hook #9672 for this fly. The body is medium flat silver tinsel. The underwing is either yellow hackle or a sparse bunch of yellow calftail.

On each side of the fly a Mallard flank feather is tied in and the tips are slightly lacquered and stroked to a point. The hackle is wound in the conventional dry fly manner. There has been much controversy as to how this fly should be classified. It seems to work well as a streamer, wet fly and even a dry fly. Personally I fish it dry until it sinks, then I fish it as a streamer.

100 **HOWARD SPECIAL** I recommend a Mustad hook #79580. This fly was developed by the late Herb Howard and became one of his favorites. It is extremely easy to tie.

100 **LIGHT SPRUCE** I recommend a Mustad hook #9672 for this fly. This fly is tied in the exact same manner as the Dark Spruce Streamer but, instead of a furnace wing, the Light Spruce fly has a light badger hackle wing. The collar is also of light badger hackle.

100 **LITTLE BROOK TROUT** For this fly I use a Mustad hook #79580. The tail of this fly is two layers of hackle fibers—the bottom red, the top green. The wing is tied in the following manner: first, a sparse layer of white bucktail; directly over this another sparse layer of orange bucktail; over this a layer of green bucktail; and finally a layer of natural gray squirrel. The throat is of orange hackle.

101 **LITTLE BROWN TROUT** I use a Mustad hook #79580 for this pattern. The tail for this fly can either be a ginger hackle trimmed to a "V" shape and tied in, or several ginger hackle fibers tied short. Over this, sparse orangish bucktail and over this, dark red squirrel tail.

101 **LITTLE RAINBOW TROUT** I recommend a Mustad hook #79580 for this pattern. The tail can either be green bucktail or green hackle fibers. The underwing is sparse white bucktail. Directly over this is a sparse bunch of pink bucktail and over this a top of natural brown bucktail dyed green. The throat of this fly is a small bunch of either pink bucktail or pink calftail tied short.

101 **MAGOG SMELT** I use a Mustad hook #79580 for this fly. The tail of this fly calls for a bunch of teal flank fibers, but if not available, a finely speckled guinea hen feather or a thickly barred Mallard can be used. The wing of this fly is a sparse white bucktail underwing. Over this some sparse yellow bucktail and over this a sparse bunch of light violet bucktail. The top is six or eight peacock herls. The cheeks of this fly should be teal, but if not available, use strongly barred Mallard.

101 **MARABOU MUDDLER, White** A Mustad hook #79580 is used for this fly. Tying instructions for the mylar body of this fly are given under the Black Marabou pattern. Where the body ends behind the eye I tie in a bunch of white marabou one half again as long as the body. Over this goes a topping of three or four peacock herls. The fly is finished off with a spun deer hair collar with head trimmed to shape. For the color combinations, a yellow, black, brown, olive or gray marabou wing may be used.

101 **MARABOU STREAMER, Yellow** For this fly I use a Mustad hook #79580. When tying in the red wool tail a good trick to learn is to tie in the wool at the wing position and keep it at the top of the hook shank, binding the wool down all the way

to the bend of the hook and then bringing the thread back to the original tie-in position. Now clip the tail to proper length and tie in the tinsel. Running the wool the entire length of the body will enable you to wind a smooth tinsel body. There are many different kinds of marabou streamers. Other popular colors are white, black, and brown and white.

101 **MICKEY FINN** I use a Mustad hook #79580 for this pattern. The body of this classic fly is medium flat silver tinsel with a medium oval tinsel rib. The underwing, or first layer of hair, is dyed yellow bucktail. The middle layer section is dyed red bucktail and over this another layer of dyed yellow bucktail. Take care in keeping the total wing as sparse as possible, while keeping the color definition very distinct. An eye can be painted on the head of this fly, but is optional.

101 **MOOSE RIVER** The hook for this fly should be a Mustad #79580. The wing of this fly consists of a sparse bunch of white bucktail tied in half as long again as the body. The overwing is four light badger saddle hackles and over this a topping of five or six peacock herls.

101 **MUDDLER MINNOW** I use a Mustad hook #79580. The underwing is a bunch of natural gray squirrel hair. (Make sure when tying in the underwing that you leave enough room for the head.) On each side of this underwing tie in matched sections of mottled brown turkey wing feathers. Spin a collar of natural deer hair and trim it to shape, leaving the natural tips long to form a collar around the body. The Western dry-fly variation of this fly calls for a white calftail underwing in

place of the squirrel. If you are planning on deep fishing with this fly, I recommend you clip the head as closely as possible as a large amount of deer hair tends to make the fly very buoyant. It can also be weighted with lead wire around the shank before the body is wound.

101 **NINE-THREE** I use either a Mustad hook #79580 or #9575. The original pattern calls for the four green hackles to be tied flat over the body and the black hackles to be tied in directly over the green hackles. However, the preferred method now is to tie all of the hackles in the conventional streamer wing manner.

101 **PROFESSOR** I prefer a Mustad hook #79580. The tail of this fly calls for a thin section of red goose quill, but long red hackle fibers may be used. The wing is natural gray squirrel tail and should be tied very long. A helpful hint when using squirrel tail is to select the amount you need and then pull the hairs back from the skin at a 90 degree angle before clipping them off. After clipping them off, you will notice how evenly the natural markings are aligned.

102 **RAINBOW TROUT (Thunder Creek)** The hook should be a Mustad #36620. This fly is tied in the exact manner as given for the **Black Nose Dace (Thunder Creek)**. The only difference is that the lateral stripe is tied from dyed pink bucktail and the back is formed from natural brown bucktail dyed green.

102 **RED & WHITE BUCKTAIL** I prefer using a Mustad hook #79580. The body of this fly is medium flat silver tinsel with an oval tinsel rib. The underwing is white bucktail tied sparse, and over this is red bucktail tied sparse. Top with three or four peacock herls slightly longer than the bucktail wing.

102 **ROYAL COACHMAN** The hook I prefer for this fly is a Mustad #79580. The body of this fly is tied in the same manner as that of the dry fly Royal Coachman except that the middle floss section is much longer. The wing is four matched white saddle or neck hackles.

102 **SILVER DARTER** For this fly I use a Mustad hook #79580. The tail of this fly is a thin section of silver pheasant wing. The wing should be of the whitest badger you have. The throat is tied from four or five strands of peacock sword feather.

102 **SILVER SHINER (Thunder Creek)** I use a Mustad hook #36620 for this fly. This fly is tied in the same manner as the **Black Nose Dace (Thunder Creek)** except the black lateral section is omitted and the black stripe painted on the head is not used.

102 **SPUDDLER** The hook I use is a Mustad #79580. The tying thread is brown. The tail is brown calftail. The rear three-fourths of the body is cream wool. The front one-fourth of the body is red wool. The underwing of this fly is brown calftail tied in extending to the hook bend. Over this are two grizzly hackles dyed brown and tied in flat over the underwing. Over this is a bunch of red fox squirrel tail tied one-half as long as the grizzly wing. The head is spun antelope hair clipped to a flat torpedo shape.

102 **SUPERVISOR** I prefer a Mustad hook #79580. The underwing is a small bunch of white bucktail. The

wing is tied directly over and consists of four saddle hackles dyed silver doctor blue (robin's egg blue). On each side of this, tie in one supervisor green (grass green) saddle hackle tip half as long as the blue wing. Over the entire wing, a topping of five or six peacock herls is used.

102 **WARDEN'S WORRY** I use a Mustad hook #79580 for this fly. The tail is a thin section of red goose primary. The body can be either yellowish orange fur or wool of the same coloration. The rib should be medium oval gold tinsel but flat tinsel will also do. The wing is of natural brown bucktail.

102 **WESTERN BLACK GHOST** For this fly I use a Mustad hook #7948A. The tail is yellow hackle fibers. For the rib I use medium oval silver tinsel. The wing is a healthy bunch of white bucktail. The collar is tied in directly in front of the wing from a large dyed black cock hackle.

102 **YELLOW BREECHES** I use a Mustad hook #79580. The body is tied exclusively from oval silver tinsel. The underwing is yellow marabou one-half again as long as the body. The overwing is an equal amount of brown marabou tied the same length as the yellow. On each side of this wing tie in three or four peacock herls as a lateral stripe. This stripe should cover where the brown and yellow marabou meet.

New Patterns
NYMPHS

103 **EMERGER** This is one of the most versatile patterns developed by Swisher and Richards. It is usually tied on a regular Mustad wet-fly hook #9671 or #3906, but since the authors also recommend it for fishing directly in the surface film, one should also carry a supply of emergers on light-wire dry-fly hooks such as the Mustad #94833 or #94840. There are also several variations of shades aside from the medium brown suggested in the material list, like tan or olive. Don't be afraid to tie some big ones in size 2 and 4, or even some very small 24s. They all work well at one time or another during a fly hatch. For wings I prefer hen-hackle tips as they are "fuller" than rooster hackle.

103 **FLOATING CADDIS PUPA** The combined effort of two Scandinavian anglers, Preben Trop Jacobsen and Ken Bostrom, produced this effective pattern. They had discovered that some caddis species had a very peculiar method of hatching. They would rise to the surface and swim to shore, rather than hatching in the conventional manner on the water surface like most other caddis. The fly is fairly simple. It should be dressed on a dry-fly hook like Mustad #94833 or 94840. The black hackle on the posterior end of the pupa is usually trimmed before it is wound, but that is a matter of preference. The main hackle, representing the legs, is wound first and then trimmed almost flush with the underbody. I prefer to make the body of Seal-Ex, even though that material was not designed for dry-fly dubbing, for the translucency makes it very desirable. It must be treated well with some dry-fly flotant before it is fished. It is not a dry fly, but a pupa that is fished dry.

104 **JORGENSEN'S LATEX STONE FLY NYMPH** This nymph is one of my favorites, and I designed it especially to imitate some of the large stone fly nymphs of the West. I use a Mustad #3665A, 6X long, or a #38941, 3X long. Since stone-fly nymphs are usually somewhat flat, it will require some sort of underbody attached on the hook-shank before the dubbing is applied. I use either a strip of lead wire on each side of the shank, or a piece of thin plastic trimmed to shape. Thin lead wire can then be wound over the plastic if extra weight is needed. The tails and feelers are fibers taken from the leading edge of turkey-wing pointers that have been dyed dark brown. For ribbing I sometimes use heavy cotton thread instead of stripped quill. The special features of these nymphs are the wingcases made of latex and tinted with a waterproof marking pen. The section dealing with basic tying procedures shows a photograph of the actual shape of the wingcases before they are tied in. The nymph can be dressed in any size and color.

104 **LATEX CADDIS LARVA** The hook I normally use is a Mustad #3906 or #3906B, but it has lately become fashionable to dress this type of artificial on an English bait hook, Mustad #37160, which has a curved shank. The latex strips for the body are cut with a razor blade drawn along a ruler, or with a simple paper cutter. The strips should be anywhere from one-eighth to one-sixteenth inch wide, depending on the size larva being dressed. When winding the latex, you should only apply moderate pull and stretch on the material to bring out the segmentation. The latex body can be left natural creamy, or tinted any color with waterproof marking pen. The naturals that you are imitating

are found on the bottom of the stream, and the artificial should be weighted with some .010 lead wire before the body is applied.

104 **SOLOMON CADDIS PUPA** The same hooks I recommended for the Latex Caddis Larva can be used for this type of pupa. If you use a Mustad #3906 or #3906B, the body should be started well down on the bend to get the desired shape. The mallard quill strips used to imitate the wings should be sprayed with a clear lacquer like Krylon before they are tied in as they may otherwise split. The pupa can be tied in many different colors to suit the local conditions. I prefer Seal-Ex for the body, and prepare it in a loop or simply roll it on the tying thread like making an ordinary dubbing.

104 **WIGGLE NYMPH** I first saw this type of fly many years ago when Bill Blades designed some very lively stone-fly nymphs dressed on two sections of brass tubing. This type, however, is dressed on two hooks. The front one is a Mustad #3906 and the rear is a Mustad Aberdeen #3261 with a ringed eye. I first dress the abdomen (rear portion) on the Aberdeen hook, then tie in some ten to fifteen-pound-test monofilament or fine stainless piano wire on the #3906 that will serve as a hinge between the two hooks. Thread the eye of the rear hook on the hinge material, then double it and tie it down again on the #3906 hook. Make the hinge loop as small as you can, but make sure the abdomen portion is able to move freely. Now finish the front of the nymph in the usual manner. Any type of nymph can be dressed by this method, particularly the very large ones like the green drake and the Michigan may fly nymph. Choose the hook sizes to match the size insect being dressed.

WET FLIES

103 **MORSE'S ALDER FLY**   This fly was designed by Bob Morse—a Catskill fly tyer of note. It is tied on a Mustad #3906 hook. The unusual construction of body and wing is very unique. Take a bunch of long hair, at least two inches in length for a size 10 hook and tie it on in front of the shank, close to the eye. The hair tips should project forward over the eye and be as long as the hook length when folded back. Now wind the tying thread back down to the bend, binding the hair down on the shank in the process. Continue to wind over it until you reach slightly down on the bend. Take some extra tight turns at that point. Wind the tying thread toward the front one eighth inch. Now gather the hair ends into a tight bunch and hold them tightly forward over the hook shank and hold them while winding the tying thread over them and again binding them down on the shank. This forms the first segment of the body. From that tie-down point, wind the tying thread another one eighth inch toward the front, binding the hair down on the shank. Double the hair back and hold it while again winding over it to the rear, binding down the hair. When the thread winding reaches directly in front of the first segment you have formed, wind it back to directly in front of the one-eighth-inch segment you formed with hair and tying thread. Fold the hair bunch forward over the segment and tie it down as you did the first one, and the second section of the body is finished. Continue to form the rest of the body and when you reach the front, cut the surplus, fold the hair tips back over the body to form the wing and your fly is finished.

103 **PHEASANT TAIL**   I use a Mustad #3906 or #3906B for this simple but very effective fly. The copper wire is tied in first. If the fly is to be fished very deep, it's best to attach some .010 lead wire before the body is applied. I usually get a complete pheasant tail so I have a good selection of feathers to choose from. In this case I seek out a center tail with the longest and strongest fibers. You will need about six to eight fibers to form the body. Tie them in by the tips and then twist them together before you wind them on the shank. I often apply a little cement on the shank first. The copper wire is now wound counter-clockwise, which prevents it from sinking into the pheasant fibers and also adds strength to the body. The partridge feather can be wound whole, as it is, or stripped off on one side.

103 **STARLING HERL**   This is one of the most popular soft-hackle flies, and like the Pheasant Tail fly it is dressed on a Mustad #3906 or #3906B. The peacock herl body is easy to make. I use two or three herls, depending on the size fly I am dressing. Since this type of herl is very fragile, I strengthen it by forming a thread loop at the bend where the herl is tied in and twist it in with the herl before it is wound on the hook. Apply a little cement on the shank before winding the body to further add to the strength. The starling feather that is used for the hackle sits on the shoulder of the wing. It is a small feather with a whitish tip.

103 **TUP'S INDISPENSABLE**   This is another soft-hackle fly but with a
thorax (the pinkish fur tied on in
front of the floss). While the dressing calls for an ordinary soft pale
blue-dun hackle, Sylvester Nemes,
the author of *The Soft Hackle Fly*,
mentions that he also dresses one
with a partridge hackle that is dyed
a blue-dun shade, and that it works
better that way in some areas.

DRY FLIES

103 **COLORADO KING**   I use a Mustad
dry-fly hook #94833 or #94840 for
this important western fly. The tail
fibers are peccary (wild pig) but actually any very stiff hair can be
used. The important thing is that
they are tied splayed so they act as
outriggers and aid the fly in balanc-
ing. The palmer hackle can also be
trimmed a little underneath if it is
riding too high. On smaller sizes
you can change the greyish-brown
elk hair to calf tail, which is somewhat softer. The fly works very well
in the East when caddis flies are on
the water.

103 **DIVING CADDIS FLY**   This unusual fly was introduced to me by
my friend the Swedish angler Ken
Bostrom. It's a very simple fly tied
on a Mustad dry-fly hook #98433.
The body is dubbed with ordinary
poly-dubbing, and the wing is a
whole strand of poly yarn tied in
like you would when dressing a
spent wing. When the yarn is fastened, both wings are held back and
secured to form a slanting back and
slightly divided caddis fly wing.
Trim the wing to the length seen in
the color photograph. It is necessary
to apply a little dubbing in front
after the wing is secured to form a
head and cover the thread wind-

ings. When the fly is finished it
should be well soaked in dry-fly
flotant. It is fished by casting across
and slightly upstream. When it hits
the water it is gently pulled under
like a caddis diving to deposit the
eggs. Give it slack line and it will
rise to the surface. Do this a couple
of times; it drives the fish wild.

103 **HEN SPINNER**   This type of spinner was made popular by Swisher
and Richards a few years ago, and
got its name from the type of feathers used for the wings. Since it floats
in the fur body rather than on a
hackle I prefer to use a Mustad up-
eyed dry-fly hook #94842, but you
can of course also use the regular
Mustad #94833 if you wish. When
tying in the wings one must be careful to set them very straight or they
will act as a propellor and spin the
leader. The tails consist of some
very stiff hackle fibers tied splayed
in a V shape so they will act as outriggers and aid the fly in staying
afloat. There are many different
combinations of these spinners, all
with light-gray wings but with
bodies in dark olive, light olive,
reddish-brown, and other colors.
The tails are then usually kept in a
slightly lighter shade than the body
color.

103 **JORGENSEN HACKLE SPINNER**   I
use a Mustad up-eyed dry-fly hook
#94842 for this fly. The abdomen
(rear body portion) is made as an
extension type from a brown rooster
hackle with the fibers reversed and
set in cement. The two tails are fibers that remain after the hackle tip
is trimmed away. One fiber is left on
each side of the stem. To strengthen
those, I generally apply a little cement. After the abdomen is completed and tied in, I fasten a narrow

brown quill section (turkey wing will do nicely) with the longest portion projecting toward the rear. This quill section will later become the top of the front body portion (thorax). I now tie in a pale blue-dun rooster hackle with fibers that are as long as from the hook-eye to the tip of the abdomen. Tie in the hackle in front of the abdomen and wind it like an ordinary dry-fly hackle. Tie it off in front and divide all the fibers above and below into two equal bunches. Each bunch is now tied spent wing by winding tying thread directly around each bunch separately. Apply a little cement on the windings and press on the fibers with your fingers to flare them out a little. Now fold the quill section forward over the top between the two wings and tie it down in front. Trim away the surplus and wind a small head before applying a little cement, which finishes the spinner. They can be dressed in all sizes and colors to suit your needs.

103 **SKATER** There are several types of skaters. The one I have included is the simplest. I tie it on a Mustad dry-fly hook #94833 or a short-shank spider hook, Mustad #9523. The hackles are tied in by the butt ends all at the same time, but they are wound on the shank one at a time. When the fly is finished I apply a little cement on the head and directly behind the hackles, which should be tightly pressed together on the shank. Another version of a skater is the original by Hewitt, but that one is considerably more complicated to dress. In any event, the one I have just described works just as well.

103 **STILLBORN** Imitations of the different stages of may flies are many and varied. The stillborn is a very recent observation by Swisher and Richards, although I am told by the Danish angler-author Preben Torp Jacobsen that they have been experimenting with that type of artificial for some time in Europe. I tie the fly on a Mustad dry-fly hook #94842. The abdomen is of the extension, reversed hackle type described under the **Jorgensen Hackle Spinner**. The thorax fur is applied in front of the abdomen before the wings are attached. The position of the wings is quite clear when you study the photograph. They are fastened a little down on each side of the thorax portion and are curving out and away from each other. I usually tie in both wings at the same time. If you have difficulty in preventing the quill sections from splitting, I can recommend that you spray them with clear Krylon first.

STREAMERS

104 **JORGENSEN'S STREAKER** When brown-mottled turkey wing quills suddenly became scarce, I decided to design a "naked" muddler. It is tied on a Mustad #38941, 3X long streamer hook. The hair is applied in the same manner as explained in the section with basic tying instructions, "The Muddler Minnow." The trimming is the most important thing to observe. First I trim away all the hair underneath, very close to the hook-shank, then I trim the sides, keeping the scissor blades one eighth of an inch away from the shank, doing both sides the same way. The head should have a gentle taper. The top is trimmed in a curve, all the way from the rear to the eye as can clearly be seen in the photograph. The longest hair left should

reach to the bend or just slightly beyond. They are also extremely effective when tied in other colors like olive and black.

104 **LLAMA FLY** Eric Leiser of the Rivergate in Cold Spring, New York, designed this fly. He recommends that it be tied on a Mustad hook #79580. Due to the shortness of ground hog guard hair one is limited to a size 8 and down. When applying the hairwing one should put a little cement on the butt ends to prevent them from tearing out.

104 **MATUKA** Matukas are very old New Zealand flies that have become very popular in this country in the last few years. I dress them on either Mustad #79580, 4X long or #38941, 3X long. It's best to use very wide webby hen or saddle hackles for those flies. Tie in the ribbing and apply the body material first. If you wish to add some extra weight to get them down deep, you can wind some lead wire on the shank before the body is dressed. Now select two to four hackles so that they are of the same size and tie them in together at the head in front of the finished body portion. Grasp the hackles together and hold them tightly and directly over the body in an upright position. Now separate the fibers at the place where the first turn of ribbing is to be applied. Take a turn of ribbing around the body, tying the hackle stems down on top in the process. Continue this procedure when spiraling the ribbing over the entire body to the front. Tie it off and trim the surplus

ribbing. The hackle is tied on in front by the tip and doubled as it is being wound as a collar. There is no limit to the color combinations one can use. The most popular are the furnace and badger hackles. But a grizzly dyed olive is perhaps the deadliest of them all.

104 **MATUKA SCULPIN** These artificials are not easy to tie and should not be attempted until you have considerable experience in tying with deer hair. The hook I use is a Mustad #38941, 3X long. Start the fly by tying in the ribbing, body, and feathers as explained for the ordinary Matuka. Make sure that you leave a third of the hook shank free in front to accommodate the head. Next tie in the pectoral fins that sit vertically and curving outward on each side. Apply a little cement on the windings before proceeding. Now apply a small bunch of natural deer-body hair and hold it under the shank when it is being flared up. Next apply a similar bunch of hair dyed golden brown and hold it on top when it is being fastened directly above the first bunch. In this manner you are making a head that is lighter underneath than on top. Cut a small bunch of black-dyed deer-body hair and apply it in the middle of the golden brown hair on top, then proceed with the light underneath and another bunch of golden brown on top until the entire space in front is filled with packed hair. Trim the head to shape as seen in the color photograph and the fly is finished.

5

MODERN
TROUT FLIES
in COLOR

THE 240 FULL-COLOR PHOTOGRAPHS THAT FOLLOW ARE OF THE MOST popular trout flies used today. In all instances, I tied the flies from what I believe to be the original and classic patterns. Also included are many new and productive patterns that are of significant value to the complete fly fisher. The very newest patterns are included at the end.

Since all natural insects vary in coloration from stream to stream and from region to region, these photographs must be used as a guideline—not a bible. I heartily encourage you to experiment with these patterns in an attempt to get closer to regional variations—and also to develop the creativity that makes fly fishing and fly tying the never-ending challenge we all love.

BAETIS NYMPH 43

14 to 22	hook	8 to 18, sproat
Olive	thread	Brown
Gray fibers	tail	None
Brownish gray fur, dark gray rib	body	Dirty white spun fur
None	thorax	brown fur
Gray hen	legs	Brown fur and guard hairs
Gray goose	wing case	None

44 CADDIS LARVA, WHITE ▶

BITCH CREEK 43

4 to 6, 6X long	hook	8 to 16, sproat
Black	thread	Tan
Rubber hackle	tail	None
Orange chenille bottom, black top, rubber hackle feelers	body	Cream fur
Black chenille	thorax	Tan fur collar
Brown hackle	legs	Tan fur with guard hairs
None	wing case	Mallard quill on sides

CADDIS PUPA, CREAM ▶

BLUE QUILL NYMPH 43

(*Adoptiva*)

16, 18	hook	8 to 16, sproat
Black	thread	Brown
Pheasant fibers	tail	None
Yellow-brown fur	body	Brown spun fur
None	thorax	Brown fur collar
Ginger hen	legs	Partridge
Black crow	wing case	Mallard quill on sides

44 CADDIS PUPA, BROWN ▶

BLUE-WINGED OLIVE NYMPH 44

14 to 16	hook	8 to 16, sproat
Olive	thread	Brown
Wood-duck	tail	None
Gray-brown fur, brown rib	body	Green spun fur
Same as body, no rib	thorax	Brown fur collar
Brown partridge	legs	Partridge and brown fur with guard hairs
Black crow	wing case	None, mallard quill on sides

CADDIS PUPA, GREEN ▶

CADDIS LARVA, OLIVE 44

8 to 18, sproat	hook	8 to 16
Olive	thread	Brown
None	tail	None
Dirty olive green, spun fur	body	Gray spun fur
Brown fur	thorax	Brown fur collar
Brown fur and guard hairs	legs	Partridge and brown fur with guard hairs
	wing case	None, mallard quill on sides

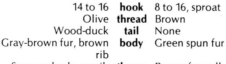

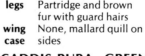

CADDIS PUPA, GRAY ▶

◄
CAENIS NYMPH, FUR 44

20 to 28	**hook**	1 to 14
Brown	**thread**	Black
Dark pheasant (3)	**tail**	None
Grayish-tan fur, tan rib	**body**	Gray fur, gray squirrel tail wing
Thick grayish-tan fur	**thorax**	None
None	**legs**	None
Black	**wing case**	None

45 **FLEDERMAUS**
►

◄
CASUAL DRESS 44

4 to 10, 3X long	**hook**	8 4X long
Black	**thread**	Olive
Muskrat fur	**tail**	Light mini-herl, stripped.
Spun muskrat fur, muskrat collar, black ostrich herl head	**body**	Tan-olive fur, olive rib
None	**thorax**	None
None	**legs**	Wood-duck flank
None	**wing case**	Mottled turkey

45 **GREEN DRAKE**
(*Ephemera guttulata*)
►

◄
CATSKILL CURLER, YELLOW 44

6 to 12, 4X long	**hook**	8 to 14
Brown monocord	**thread**	Black
Two matched peccary fibers (long-heavy)	**tail**	Brown fibers
Yellow wool with brown mono rib	**body**	Hare's ear fur, gold tinsel rib
Partridge or grouse clumped	**thorax**	Same as body, no rib
Yellow wool, brown fur collar	**legs**	Picked out body fur
Grouse body feathers (2)	**wing case**	Mallard quill

45 **HARE'S EAR, GOLD RIBBED**
►

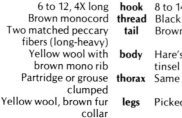

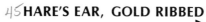

◄
CRESS BUG, FUR 45

8 to 20	**hook**	2 to 6, 6X long
Olive	**thread**	black
None	**tail**	Brown fibers, short
Medium olive-brown fur, spun, trimmed flat and oval	**body**	Blackish-brown fur, black rib, gills of brown hackle tied palmer, trimmed
None	**thorax**	Spun gray fur
None	**legs**	None, turkey mandibles
None	**wing case**	Dark turkey

45 **HELGRAMMITE**
►

◄
DUN VARIANT NYMPH 45
(*Flick*)

10	**hook**	12 to 16, 2X long
Olive	**thread**	Olive
Peacock herl short	**tail**	Wood-duck flank
Claret seal and black wool mixed	**body**	Gray-brown fur, brown rib
None	**thorax**	Same as body, no rib
Grouse hackle	**legs**	Brown partridge
None	**wing case**	Dark brown turkey

46 **HENDRICKSON**
(*Ephemerella subvaria*)
►

ISONYCHIA NYMPH 46
(*Bi-color*)

12, 4X long	**hook**	6 to 10, 4X long
Brown	**thread**	Tan
Pheasant tail	**tail**	Gray mini ostrich herl (3)
Claret seal and brown fur, tan rib	**body**	Grayish-tan fur, picked out gills
Same as body, no rib	**thorax**	None
Grouse hackle	**legs**	None
Natural dark goose quill	**wing case**	Dark brown fur, lacquered

MICHIGAN MAY FLY, FUR ▶

LEAD-WING COACHMAN 46

12	**hook**	18 to 28
Brown	**thread**	Gray
Dark brown fibers	**tail**	None
Peacock herl, black with rib	**body**	Muskrat fur
None	**thorax**	None
Coachman brown hackle	**legs**	None
Black quill strip (optional)	**wing case**	None

46 **MIDGE PUPA, GRAY** ▶

LEPTOPHLEBIA NYMPH 46

10 to 18	**hook**	18 to 28
Black	**thread**	Brown
Gray ostrich mini-herl (3)	**tail**	None
Stripped peacock quill, gray duck quill wing	**body**	Cream fur
Gray fur	**thorax**	Peacock herl head
Gray hen hackle	**legs**	None
Gray duck	**wing case**	None

46 **MIDGE PUPA, CREAM** ▶

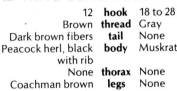

MARCH BROWN, FLICK 46

10	**hook**	4 to 14, 4X long
Brown	**thread**	Black
Pheasant fibers	**tail**	Crow fibers
Amber seal and red fox, brown rib	**body**	Black chenille rear
None	**thorax**	Yellow chenille
Partridge brown	**legs**	Black hackle
Pheasant tail	**wing case**	Black chenille

47 **MONTANA NYMPH** ▶

MARCH BROWN, POUL'S

10 to 14, 2X long	**hook**	16 to 20
Brown	**thread**	Black
Pheasant tail fibers (3)	**tail**	Grizzly fibers
Brownish yellow fur	**body**	Light and dark moose mane
Gray	**thorax**	Peacock herl
Dark ginger hackle	**legs**	Grizzly fiber antennae
Dark turkey section	**wing case**	None

47 **MOSQUITO LARVA** ▶

◀
MUSKRAT 47

8 to 14, 2X long	**hook**	12 to 18
Black	**thread**	Olive
None	**tail**	None
Muskrat fur	**body**	Medium olive-brown fur spun and trimmed top and sides
Black ostrich herl	**thorax**	None
Guinea hen fibers (optional)	**legs**	Untrimmed fur
None	**wing case**	None (top of fly should be lacquered)

47 **SHRIMP, FUR**
▶

◀
OLIVE DUN 47

14 to 18	**hook**	10 to 12, 3X long
Brown	**thread**	Olive
3 pheasant tails	**tail**	Pheasant tails (3)
Dark olive-gray fur, brown rib	**body**	Reddish-tan fur
Same as body, no rib	**thorax**	None
Light brown hen hackle	**legs**	None
Gray goose primary section	**wing case**	Gray-tan fur

47 **STENONEMA, FUR**
▶

◀
OTTER 47

8 to 14	**hook**	6 to 12, 4X long
Black	**thread**	Yellow
Mallard Flank	**tail**	Tan hackle stems, stripped
Otter belly fur	**body**	Amber seal fur, gold cotton rib
None	**thorax**	None
Light dun hen hackle	**legs**	Tan variant hen hackle
Mallard Flank	**wing case**	Two, mottled turkey

48 **STONE FLY, POUL'S**
▶

◀
POTAMANTHUS NYMPH 47
(*Distinctus*)

12, 3X long	**hook**	8-12, 2X long
Tan	**thread**	Primrose
Wood-duck	**tail**	Pheasant fibers (2)
Tan and amber fur, tan ribbing	**body**	Ginger hackle stem and amber seal fur
None	**thorax**	None
Creamy tan hen	**legs**	Grouse hackle
Gray quill strip	**wing case**	Wood-duck flank

48 **STONE FLY CREEPER, FLICK**
▶

◀
QUILL GORDON, FUR 47

12 to 14	**hook**	1 to 8, 4X long
Olive	**thread**	Brown
Pheasant fibers (2)	**tail**	Peccary (2)
Olive-brown fur	**body**	Black and brown fur, brown rib
None	**thorax**	Same
None	**legs**	Grouse hackle
Dark brown fur set in cement	**wing case**	Brown turkey (2)

48 **STONE FLY, LARGE BLACK**
▶

◄ SULPHUR NYMPH, FUR 48

16 to 18	**hook**	12 and 14
Tan or gray	**thread**	Black
Pheasant fibers	**tail**	Mallard flank
Tan and dark ginger fur	**body**	Gray fur, yellow chenille egg sac
None	**thorax**	
None	**legs**	
	hackle	Medium brown hen
	wing	Gray duck quill
Grayish-brown fur set in cement	**wing case**	

49 BEAVERKILL, FEMALE ►

◄ TELLICO NYMPH 48

8 to 16	**hook**	8 to 14
Black	**thread**	Black
Brown fibers	**tail**	None
Yellow floss, peacock rib	**body**	Black chenille
None	**thorax**	
Brown hackle	**legs**	
	hackle	Black hen
	wing	Gray duck quill
Peacock herl over entire body	**wing case**	

49 BLACK GNAT ►

◄ ZUG BUG 48

6 to 16, 2X long	**hook**	12 and 14
Black	**thread**	Black
3 peacock swords	**tail**	Blue dun hackle fibers
Peacock herl, silver rib	**body**	Peacock quill
Same as body, no rib	**thorax**	
Brown hackle	**legs**	
	hackle	Blue dun hen
	wing	Dark gray duck quill
Mallard flank, flat, clipped	**wing case**	

49 BLACK QUILL ►

WET FLIES

◄ ALDER 48

10 to 14	**hook**	2 to 14
Black	**thread**	Red or black
None	**tail**	Red wool butt, short
Peacock herl, gold tag	**body**	Black chenille
Black hen	**hackle**	Grizzly palmer
Mottled turkey	**wing**	None

49 BLACK WOOLY WORM ►

◄ ALEXANDRA 49

6 to 10	**hook**	10 to 18
Black	**thread**	Black
Peacock sword, red feather	**tail**	Medium blue dun
Silver, oval rib	**body**	Gray fur
Black	**hackle**	Blue dun hen
Peacock sword, red feather	**wing**	Gray duck quill

49 BLUE DUN ►

◀
BLUE-WINGED OLIVE 49

14 to 24	hook	8 to 14
Olive	thread	Yellow
Gray Fibers	tail	Wood-duck
Olive fur	body	Cream fur
Medium blue dun	hackle	Light·ginger hen
Gray duck quill	wing	Wood-duck flank

49 **CAHILL, LIGHT** ▶

◀
BREADCRUST 49

8 to 14	hook	2 to 10
Orange	thread	Black
None	tail	Pheasant breast
Orange wool, stripped quill rib	body	Chenille, silver rib
Grizzly	hackle	Ring-neck flank
None	wing	None

50 **CAREY SPECIAL** ▶

◀
BROWN HACKLE 49

8 to 14	hook	10 to 14
Black	thread	Black
Red floss	tail	None
Peacock herl	body	Claret chenille
Brown	hackle	Hen, dyed claret
None	wing	Dark gray duck quill

50 **CLARET GNAT** ▶

◀
BROWN WOOLY WORM 49

6 to 10	hook	12 to 14
Red or black	thread	Black
Red wool butt	tail	None
Brown chenille	body	Peacock herl
Grizzly palmer	hackle	Brown
None	wing	White duck quill

50 **COACHMAN** ▶

◀
CAHILL, DARK 49

8 to 14	hook	8 to 12
Brown	thread	Black
Brown fibers	tail	Gold pheas. Tippets
Gray fur	body	Peacock herl, yellow floss center
Brown hen	hackle	Yellow hen
Wood-duck flank	wing	White duck quill

50 **COACHMAN, CALIFORNIA** ▶

◄
COACHMAN, LEAD WING 50

10 to 14	hook	12 to 14
Black	thread	Black
None	tail	Ginger fibers
Peacock herl, flat gold tinsel tag	body	Peacock quill
Dark brown	hackle	Ginger hen
Dark gray duck quill	wing	Gray duck quill

GINGER QUILL
►

◄
COACHMAN, ROYAL 50

8 to 14	hook	6 to 4, 3X long
Black	thread	Tan
Tippet fibers	tail	Turkey dyed gold
Peacock herl, red floss, herl	body	Gold wool and rib
Brown	hackle	Gold, gold teal forward
White duck quill	wing	Bucktail dyed gold

51 ## GOLDEN STONE
►

◄
COWDUNG 50

10 to 14	hook	10 to 14
Black	thread	Black
None, gold tinsel tag	tail	Olive fibers (optional)
Olive green wool	body	Dark brown wool, green chenille butt
Brown hen	hackle	Brown
Brown quill	wing	Dark brown turkey tail

51 ## GRANNOM
►

◄
DARK STONE FLY 50

2 to 6, 3X long	hook	8 to 14
Black	thread	Black
Brown turkey	tail	Red wool
Tangerine wool, rib nickle-gray twist	body	Peacock herl
Dark furnace	hackle	Grizzly
Dark brown bucktail	wing	None

51 ## GRAY HACKLE
►

◄
EARLY BROWN STONE 50
(*Jennings*)

14	hook	10 to 14
Orange	thread	Olive
Pheasant fibers (2)	tail	None, gold tinsel tag
Reddish brown seal	body	Olive green floss, gold tinsel rib
Rusty dun hen	hackle	Ginger hen
2 rusty dun hackle tips, flat	wing	Dark duck quill

51 ## GREENWELL'S GLORY
►

◀ **GRIZZLY KING** 51

10 to 14	**hook**	14 to 16
Black	**thread**	White
Red feather	**tail**	Pale ginger
Green floss, gold rib	**body**	Yellowish-tan fur
Grizzly hen	**hackle**	Pale ginger hen
Mallard flank	**wing**	Pale duck quill

52 **LITTLE MARRYATT** ▶

◀ **GOLD RIBBED HARE'S EAR** 51

6 to 16	**hook**	6 to 16
Black	**thread**	Black
Brown hackle	**tail**	Red and teal
Hare's mask fur, fine gold tinsel rib	**body**	Black and yellow chenille
Picked out body fur	**hackle**	Dark brown
Mallard wing sections	**wing**	White tipped mallard quill

52 **McGINTY** ▶

◀ **HENDRICKSON, DARK** 51

10 to 14	**hook**	10 to 12
Black	**thread**	Black
Blue dun	**tail**	Brown partridge
Gray fur	**body**	Tan fur, gold rib
Blue dun	**hackle**	Brown partridge
Wood-duck flank	**wing**	Mottled turkey

52 **MARCH BROWN** ▶

◀ **HENDRICKSON, LIGHT** 51

10 to 14	**hook**	10 to 14
Tan	**thread**	Black
Blue dun	**tail**	Red duck quill
Cream fur	**body**	Claret floss, gold rib
Blue dun hen	**hackle**	Hen, dyed claret
Wood-duck flank	**wing**	Turkey quill

52 **MONTREAL** ▶

◀ **IRON BLUE DUN** 51

12 to 14	**hook**	10 to 14
Black	**thread**	White
Furnace fibers	**tail**	None
Red floss, gray fur	**body**	Yellow floss, red floss tag
Furnace hen	**hackle**	Grizzly, palmer
Dark gray duck	**wing**	Mallard flank

52 **MORMON GIRL** ▶

◀

ORANGE FISH HAWK 52

10 to 14	hook	12 to 14
Black	thread	Black
None, gold tinsel tag	tail	Blue dun
Orange floss, gold rib	body	Stripped peacock quill
Light badger	hackle	Blue dun hen
None	wing	Wood-duck

53 **QUILL GORDON** ▶

◀

PARMACHENE BELLE 52

10 to 14	hook	2 to 16
Black	thread	Black
Red and white hackle	tail	None
Yellow floss, flat silver rib	body	Black chenille, gold tag
Red and white hen	hackle	Brown hen
Red and white quill	wing	White duck quill

53 **RIO GRANDE KING** ▶

◀

PICKET PIN 53

8 to 12	hook	10 to 16
Black	thread	White
Brown fibers	tail	White fibers
Peacock herl	body	White floss, silver rib
Brown, palmer	hackle	White hen
Squirrel tail	wing	White duck quill

53 **WHITE MILLER** ▶

◀

PINK LADY 53

12 to 14	hook	12 to 14
White	thread	Black
Light ginger	tail	Ginger
Pink floss, gold rib	body	Gold tinsel, oval gold rib
Light ginger hen	hackle	Ginger, palmer
Gray duck quill	wing	Gray duck quill

53 **WICKHAMS FANCY** ▶

◀

PROFESSOR 53

12 to 14	hook	2 to 14
Black	thread	Red
Red duck quill	tail	Red wool butt
Yellow floss, gold rib	body	Yellow chenille
Dark ginger hen	hackle	Grizzly palmer
Mallard flank	wing	None

53 **YELLOW WOOLY WORM** ▶

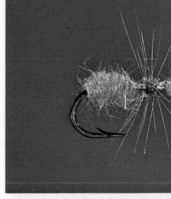

◄
ZULU 53

8 and 14	**hook**	12 to 22
Black	**thread**	Brown
Red wool	**tail**	None
Peacock herl	**body**	Golden brown fur
None	**wing**	None
Black, palmer	**hackle**	
	legs	Blue dun hackle

54 ANT, RED
►

DRY FLIES

◄
ADAMS 54

10 to 20	**hook**	10 to 22 short shank
Black	**thread**	Black
Brown and grizzly	**tail**	Badger fibers
Gray fur	**body**	Badger hackle stem
Grizzly hackle tips	**wing**	None
Brown and grizzly	**hackle**	Badger (oversize)

54 BADGER SPIDER
►

◄
ADAMS SPENT WING 54

12 to 20	**hook**	12 to 14
Black	**thread**	Black
Grizzly and brown	**tail**	Ginger
Blue gray fur	**body**	Gray fur, yellow wool butt
Grizzly	**wing**	Gray duck quill
Grizzly and brown	**hackle**	Ginger

54 BEAVERKILL, FEMALE
►

◄
ANT, BLACK 54

10 to 24	**hook**	12 to 14
Black	**thread**	Black
None	**tail**	Dark ginger
Black fur, two clumps	**body**	White floss, brown hackle, palmer
None	**wing**	Gray duck quill
Sparse black	**hackle**	Dark brown

55 BEAVERKILL, MALE
►

◄
ANT, BLACK FLYING 54

8 to 22	**hook**	10 to 14
Black	**thread**	Black
None	**tail**	None
Black fur or yarn	**body**	Black deer hair, black deer hair legs
Black hackle tips	**wing**	None
Black	**hackle**	None

55 BEETLE, BLACK
►

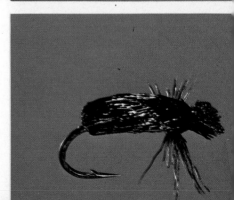

◄ BEETLE, WOOD 55

10 to 20	**hook**	12 to 20
Black	**thread**	Black
None	**tail**	Blue dun
Black deer hair, black deer hair legs and head	**body**	Stripped peacock quill
None	**wing**	Gray duck quill
None	**hackle**	Blue dun

56 BLUE QUILL ►

◄ BIRD'S STONE FLY 55

4 to 14, 4X long	**hook**	16 to 24
Orange or black	**thread**	Olive
Moose body hair	**tail**	Blue dun
Orange, furnace rib, trimmed	**body**	Yellowish olive
Brown bucktail	**wing**	Dark dun hackle points
Furnace, trimmed	**hackle**	Medium blue dun

56 BLUE-WINGED OLIVE ►

◄ BI-VISIBLE, BROWN 56

8 to 14	**hook**	16 to 18, up-eyed
Black	**thread**	Olive
Brown	**tail**	Blue dun
Brown palmer hackle	**body**	Yellowish-olive
None	**wing**	Dark blue gray
White	**hackle**	Cream badger

56 BLUE-WINGED OLIVE CUT-WING ►

◄ BLACK GNAT 56

8 to 20	**hook**	16 and 18
Black	**thread**	Yellow
Black fibers	**tail**	Pale blue dun
Black chenille	**body**	Yellow fur
Dark gray duck quill	**wing**	Pale dun, shaped
Black	**hackle**	Pale blue dun

57 BLUE-WINGED SULPHUR DUN
(*Thorax tie*)
►

◄ BLUE DUN SPIDER 56

10 to 22, short shank	**hook**	8 to 20
Black	**thread**	Black
Blue dun	**tail**	Gold. Pheas. tippets
Gray hackle stem	**body**	Peacock herl, gold tinsel tag
None	**wing**	None
Blue dun (oversized)	**hackle**	Brown

57 BROWN HACKLE ►

◄
BUCKTAIL CADDIS 57

4 to 14	hook	12 to 16
Orange or black	thread	Pale yellow
None	tail	Light ginger
Orange wool	body	Cream fur
Brown bucktail	wing	Wood-duck
Brown palmer	hackle	Light ginger

58 **CAHILL, LIGHT**
►

◄
CADDIS, DELTA WING GINGER 57

14 to 22	hook	12 to 14
Tan	thread	Black
None	tail	Brown hackle fibers
Olive-tan fur	body	Peacock herl
Tan hackle tips	wing	White goose quill
Ginger	hackle	Dark brown

58 **COACHMAN**
►

◄
CADDIS HAIR WING, GRAY 58

12 to 22	hook	8 to 12
Gray	thread	Black
None	tail	Gold. Pheas. Tippet
Gray fur	body	Peacock herl, red floss center
Gray mink tail guard hair	wing	White duck breast, matched
Blue dun	hackle	Dark brown

59 **COACHMAN, FAN WING ROYAL**
►

◄
CAENIS SPINNER, FEMALE 58

20 to 28	hook	12 and 14
Black	thread	Black
Pale blue dun fibers	tail	Brown hackle fibers
White moose mane, black fur	body	Peacock herl
White poly yarn	wing	Dark gray duck quill
None	hackle	Dark brown

59 **COACHMAN, LEAD WING**
►

◄
CAHILL, DARK 58

12 to 14	hook	10 to 20
Black	thread	Black
Dark brown fibers	tail	Gold. Pheas. Tippet
Gray fur	body	Peacock herl, red floss center
Wood-duck	wing	White duck quill
Reddish brown	hackle	Dark brown

59 **COACHMAN, ROYAL**
►

◄ **COACHMAN, ROYAL PARACHUTE** 59

10 to 16	**hook**	10 to 22, short shank
Black	**thread**	Black
Brown bucktail	**tail**	Furnace fibers
Peacock herl, red floss center	**body**	Brown hackle stem
White calf tail	**wing**	None
Brown, tied parachute	**hackle**	Furnace (oversized)

60 **FURNACE SPIDER** ►

◄ **CRANE FLY SKATER** 59

10 to 14, short up-eyed	**hook**	12 to 16
Yellow	**thread**	Brown
None	**tail**	Ginger fibers
Mallard flank, paint brown bars	**body**	Stripped peacock quill
Mallard flank	**wing**	Gray duck quill
Blue dun, parachute	**hackle**	Ginger

60 **GINGER QUILL** ►

◄ **CREAM VARIANT** 60
(*Potamanthus distinctus, Flick*)

12, short shank	**hook**	10, up-eyed
Yellow	**thread**	Yellow
Cream fibers	**tail**	Light elk mane
Cream hackle stem	**body**	Light creamy olive
None	**wing**	Mallard
Cream, size #8	**hackle**	Cream badger

60 **GREEN DRAKE CUT-WING**
(*Ephemera guttulata*) ►

◄ **DUN VARIANT** 60
(*Isonychia bicolor*)

10 to 12, short	**hook**	14
Olive	**thread**	White
Blue dun	**tail**	Dark moose mane fibers (3)
Brown hackle stem	**body**	Porcupine quill
None	**wing**	Badger and grizzly hackle, dyed dun
Dark blue dun	**hackle**	None

61 **GREEN DRAKE SPINNER**
(*Coffin fly*) ►

◄ **EPHORON SPINNER** 60

14 to 16	**hook**	12 to 16
White	**thread**	Primrose
White fibers	**tail**	Ginger fibers
White porcupine bristle	**body**	Light fawn fox
White poly yarn	**wing**	Mallard flank
None	**hackle**	Lt. grizzly and lt. ginger

61 **GRAY FOX, FLICK** ►

DRY FLIES

◄
GRAY FOX VARIANT, FLICK 61

10 to 16	**hook**	12 to 14
Primrose	**thread**	Yellow
Ginger fibers	**tail**	Pale blue dun
Cream hackle stem	**body**	Reddish brown
None	**wing**	Pale dun hackles
Ginger, lt. ginger, grizzly	**hackle**	None

62 **HENDRICKSON SPINNER** ►

◄
HENDRICKSON, DARK 61

12 to 14	**hook**	12 to 22
Black	**thread**	Gray
Wood-duck or dun fibers	**tail**	None
Reddish gray fur	**body**	Olive silk
Wood-duck	**wing**	Gray mallard over wood duck
Dark blue dun	**hackle**	Grizzly palmer, brown front

62 **HENRYVILLE SPECIAL** ►

◄
HENDRICKSON DUN 61
(*Thorax tie*)

16	**hook**	4 to 16, 3X long
Tan	**thread**	Black
Rusty blue dun	**tail**	Red fibers
Reddish brown fur	**body**	Yellow chenille, brown hackle rib, trimmed
Blue-gray, shaped	**wing**	Mottled turkey
Dark blue dun	**hackle**	Brown and grizzly

62 **HOPPER, JOE'S** ►

◄
HENDRICKSON, FEMALE 61

12 to 14	**hook**	6 to 12, 4X long
Tan	**thread**	Brown
Blue dun	**tail**	Red deer hair
Pink fox fur	**body**	Yellow orlon or wool, clipped brown palmer
Wood-duck	**wing**	Mottled turkey over yellow deer hair
Blue dun	**hackle**	Deer hair collar, clipped

62 **HOPPER, WHITLOCK** ►

◄
HENDRICKSON, LIGHT 61

12 to 14	**hook**	2 to 24
Black	**thread**	Black, yellow or red
Wood-duck or dun	**tail**	Moose body hair
Cream fox fur	**body**	Deer hair
Wood-duck	**wing**	Deer hair
Light blue dun	**hackle**	Grizzly and brown

63 **HUMPY**
(*Goofus bug*)
►

◄
HUMPY, ROYAL 63

6 to 24	hook	8 to 20
Red	thread	Black
Moose body hair	tail	None
Deer hair	body	Orange, brown hackle rib, trimmed
White calf tail	wing	Mottled turkey
Reddish-brown	hackle	Brown

64 **KING'S RIVER CADDIS**
►

◄
INCHWORM 63

12	hook	10 to 18
Green	thread	Olive green
None	tail	None
Yellow-green deer hair	body	Wing quill butt cemented to hook inside, tint yellow green, finish with nail polish
None	wing	None
None	hackle	None

64 **LEAF ROLLER**
►

◄
IRRESISTIBLE 63

4 to 14	hook	12 to 16
Black	thread	Black
Brown deer hair	tail	None
Deer hair, trimmed	body	Black fur
Brown deer hair	wing	Black crow wing section
Dark blue dun	hackle	Black deer hair collar, trimmed

64 **LETORT CRICKET**
►

◄
ISONYCHIA, CUT-WING 63

12	hook	10 to 14
Tan	thread	Yellow
Dark ginger	tail	None
Red-brown fur	body	Yellow fur, with head of natural deer hair
Blue gray	wing	Mottled turkey wing section
Dark ginger	hackle	Natural deer hair collar, trimmed

64 **LETORT HOPPER**
►

◄
JASSID 64

20 to 22	hook	10 to 12
Black	thread	Orange
None	tail	Ginger fibers
Black silk	body	Tan fur
Jungle cock, flat	wing	Wood-duck
Black	hackle	Ginger and grizzly

64 **MARCH BROWN**
►

◄ **MARCH BROWN** 64
(*Realistic*)

12 to 14	**hook**	20 to 24
Orange	**thread**	Gray
Tan	**tail**	Grizzly (optional)
Tan feather and fur	**body**	Lt. gray fur
Pheasant feather	**wing**	None
Grizzly dyed tan	**hackle**	Grizzly

65 **MIDGE, NO NAME** ►

◄ **MICHIGAN MAY FLY** 65
(*Realistic*)

10	**hook**	8 to 22
Brown	**thread**	Black
Wood-duck	**tail**	Grizzly fibers
Wood-duck, gray fur	**body**	Light and dark moose mane
Blue gray	**wing**	Grizzly hackle tips
Ginger and grizzly	**hackle**	Grizzly

65 **MOSQUITO** ►

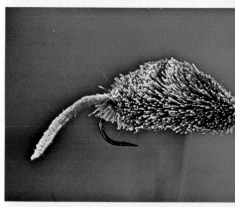

◄ **MIDGE, ADAMS** 65

20 to 28	**hook**	4, 3X long
Black	**thread**	Gray or brown
Brown and grizzly	**tail**	Strip of chamois
Gray fur	**body**	Trimmed deer hair
None	**wing**	None
Brown and grizzly	**hackle**	None

65 **MOUSE, DEER HAIR**
(*Chas. Brooks*) ►

◄ **MIDGE, BLACK** 65

18 to 22	**hook**	10 to 16
Black	**thread**	Black
Black fibers	**tail**	Gray
Black ostrich herl	**body**	Tan fur
None	**wing**	Gray duck shoulder
Black	**hackle**	None

66 **NO HACKLE, SLATE/TAN** ►

◄ **MIDGE, BLACK HERL** 65

20 to 28	**hook**	14 to 16
Black	**thread**	Yellow
Black hackle fibers	**tail**	Blue dun
Black ostrich herl	**body**	Primrose yellow
None	**wing**	Gray duck quill
None	**hackle**	Light blue dun

66 **PALE EVENING DUN** ►

◄
PALE WATERY DUN 66

14 to 16	hook	4 to 18
White	thread	Black
Pale blue dun	tail	None
Palest yellow fur	body	Peacock herl, gold tinsel tip
Pale blue dun tips	wing	None
Pale blue dun	hackle	White (front), brown (rear)

66 **RENEGADE**
►

◄
POTAMANTHUS, CUT-WING 66

12	hook	2 to 16
Yellow	thread	Black
Pale yellow	tail	Gold. Pheas. Tippet
Creamy yellow fur	body	Black chenille
Creamy yellow	wing	White duck quill
Pale yellow	hackle	Brown

66 **RIO GRANDE KING**
►

◄
POTAMANTHUS SPINNER 66

10	hook	4 to 10, 3X long
Yellow	thread	Black
Pale yellow	tail	Yellow duck quill
Pale yellow fur	body	Yellow floss
Pale blue dun	wing	Squirrel tail
None	hackle	Grizzly

67 **SOFA PILLOW, GRAY**
►

◄
QUILL GORDON 66

12 to 14	hook	10 to 24
Tan or pale yellow	thread	Black
Blue dun	tail	Moose body hair
Stripped peacock quill	body	Red floss, peacock herl
Wood-duck	wing	Badger hackle points
Medium blue dun	hackle	Badger

67 **SPRUCE FLY**
►

◄
RED QUILL 66
(*Ephemerella subvaria, male*)

12 to 14	hook	16 and 18
Black or gray	thread	Yellow
Blue dun	tail	Pale ginger
Brown hackle stem	body	Sulphur-yellow
Wood-duck	wing	Pale gray dun
Medium blue dun	hackle	Palest ginger

67 **SULPHUR DUN, CUT-WING**
►

◄
SULPHUR DUN, LITTLE 67

16 to 18	hook	6 to 16
Primrose	thread	Black
Pale ginger	tail	Brown or white calf tail
Sulphur yellow fur	body	Peacock herl, red floss center
Pale dun tips	wing	White calf tail
Pale ginger	hackle	Dark brown

67 **WULFF, ROYAL** ►

◄
SULPHUR SPINNER 67

14 to 16	hook	6 to 16
Orange	thread	White
Pale dun fibers	tail	White calf tail
Yellow-brown fur	body	Cream or white fur
Pale blue dun	wing	White bucktail
None	hackle	Cream badger

67 **WULFF, WHITE** ►

STREAMERS

◄
WULFF, BLONDE 67

4 to 14	hook	2 to 12, 4X long
Black	thread	Black
Tan elk hair	tail	Red hackle fibers
Light tan fur	body	Pale tan floss, silver rib
Tan elk hair	wing	White polar bear
Light ginger	hackle	
	throat	None
	cheeks	Jungle cock

68 **ALASKA MARY ANN** ►

◄
WULFF, GRAY 67

4 to 14	hook	4 to 12, 4X long
Black	thread	Black
Brown calf tail	tail	None
Gray fur or wool	body	Red wool, silver rib
Brown calf tail	wing	Red squirrel, reddish-brown hackle
Blue dun	hackle	
	throat	None
	cheeks	None

68 **A. S. TRUDE STREAMER** ►

◄
WULFF, GRIZZLY 67

6 to 16	hook	2 to 12, 4X long
Black	thread	Black
Brown calf tail	tail	Barred wood-duck
Pale yellow floss, lacquered	body	Embossed silver
Brown calf tail	wing	White bucktail, badger hackle
Brown and grizzly	hackle	
	throat	White bucktail
	cheeks	Barred wood duck

68 **BADGER STREAMER** ►

◄
BLACK GHOST 68

2 to 12, 6X long	**hook**	4 to 14, 3X long
Black	**thread**	Black
Yellow hackle fibers	**tail**	Peacock sword
Black floss, silver tinsel	**body**	Red floss and peacock herl
Yellow hackle	**throat**	Soft dark furnace hackle
Four white hackles	**wing**	Dark furnace hackle
Jungle cock	**cheeks**	None

69 **DARK SPRUCE**
►

◄
BLACK MARABOU 68

2 to 12, 4X long	**hook**	4 to 10, 4X long
Black	**thread**	Black
Red hackle fibers	**tail**	Pheasant tail
Black wool	**body**	Gold tinsel
Red hackle fibers	**throat**	None, black deer hair head
Black marabou	**wing**	Brown hackle and bucktail
None	**cheeks**	None

69 **DEER CREEK RAT**
►

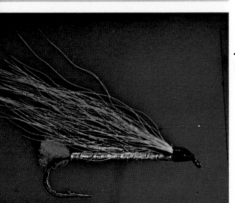

◄
BLACK NOSE DACE 68

4 to 10, 4X long	**hook**	4 to 10, 6X long
Black	**thread**	Yellow
Red yarn	**tail**	Yellow hackle, gold tag
Flat silver with oval rib	**body**	Yellow chenille
None	**throat**	Red hackle tips
White, black and brown bucktail	**wing**	Yellow-brown bucktail
None	**cheeks**	Jungle cock

69 **EDSON TIGER, DARK**
►

◄
BLACK NOSE DACE 68
(*Thunder creek*)

6, 8 and 10, 6X long	**hook**	4 to 10, 6X long
Red	**thread**	Black
None	**tail**	Gold tag & barred wood-duck
Embossed silver, white bucktail belly	**body**	Peacock herl
Red thread collar	**throat**	None
Black under brown bucktail	**wing**	Yellow bucktail, red goose topping
Yellow eye, black pupil	**cheeks**	Jungle cock

70 **EDSON TIGER, LIGHT**
►

◄
COCK-A-TOUCH 69

1 to 6, 4X long	**hook**	4 to 12, 4X long
Red	**thread**	Black
Red fibers, peacock herl tips and badger	**tail**	Red quill or bucktail
Peacock herl butts and badger hackle	**body**	Embossed silver tinsel
None	**throat**	None
None	**wing**	Black and white bucktail
None	**cheeks**	Jungle cock (optional)

70 **ESOPUS**
►

FLOATING STREAMER 70
(*Chas. Brooks*)

3/0, 4X long	hook	2 to 12, 6X long
White	thread	Black
None	tail	Silver tag
Hollow goose quill, cork plug	body	Orange floss, silver rib
Painted red-dots on body	throat	Peacock herl and bucktail
Long green marabou	wing	Green hackles, gold. pheas. topping
Yellow eye, black pupil	cheeks	Silver pheasant & jungle cock

71 **GREEN GHOST** ▶

GOLDEN DARTER 70

6 to 10, 6X	hook	6 to 10, 3X long
Black	thread	Black
Mottled turkey	tail	None
Yellow, gold rib	body	Silver tinsel
Gray jungle cock feather	throat	Grizzly hackle collar
Golden badger	wing	Mallard over yellow hackle
Jungle cock	cheeks	Jungle cock

71 **HORNBERG** ▶

GOLDEN SHINER 70
(*Thunder creek*)

6, 8 and 10, 6X long	hook	4 to 12, 4X long
Red	thread	Black
None	tail	None
Embossed gold	body	Embossed silver
White bucktail under wing	throat	None
Brown over yellow bucktail	wing	Brown hackle, yellow hackle collar
Yellow eye, black pupil	cheeks	None

71 **HOWARD SPECIAL** ▶

GRAY GHOST 71

2 to 12, 6X long	hook	2 to 10, 3X long
Black	thread	Black
Silver tag	tail	Peacock sword
Orange floss silver rib	body	Red floss, peacock herl
Peacock herl, bucktail, gold. pheas.	throat	Lt. badger hackle collar
Olive gray hackles & gold. pheas.	wing	Light badger
Silver pheasant/jungle cock	cheeks	None

71 **LIGHT SPRUCE** ▶

GREEN COSSEBOOM 71

2 to 12, 3X long	hook	2 to 12, 4X long
Red	thread	Black
Olive-green floss, silver tag	tail	Green and red
Olive-green floss, silver rib	body	Cream, silver rib
Greenish yellow hackle	throat	Orange fibers
Gray squirrel tail	wing	White, orange, green, squirrel hair over
None	cheeks	Jungle cock

71 **LITTLE BROOK TROUT** ▶

◄
LITTLE BROWN TROUT 71

2 to 12, 4X long	**hook**	2 to 10, 4X long
Black	**thread**	Black
Tan body feather	**tail**	None
White, gold rib	**body**	Silver, oval rib
None	**throat**	None
Yellow, orange hair, dark squirrel over	**wing**	Yellow and red bucktail
Jungle cock	**cheeks**	None

72 **MICKEY FINN**
▶

◄
LITTLE RAINBOW TROUT 71

2 to 12, 4X long	**hook**	2 to 6, 4X long
Black	**thread**	Black
Green	**tail**	None
Pinkish-white fur, silver tinsel rib	**body**	Flat silver tinsel
Pink	**throat**	None
White, pink, brown dyed green hair	**wing**	Peacock herl over white bucktail & badger hackle
None	**cheeks**	Gold pheasant tippet

72 **MOOSE RIVER STREAMER**
▶

◄
MAGOG SMELT 72

1 to 10, 4X long	**hook**	2 to 12, 4X long
Black	**thread**	Brown
Teal	**tail**	Mottled turkey
Silver tinsel	**body**	Flat gold tinsel
Red hackle fibers	**throat**	None
White, yellow and violet, peacock herl over	**wing**	Squirrel tail and mottled turkey
Teal	**cheeks**	Spun deer hair head, trimmed

72 **MUDDLER MINNOW**
▶

◄
MARABOU MUDDLER, WHITE 72

1/0 to 12, 4X long	**hook**	2 to 10, 6X long
Black, deer hair head	**thread**	Black
Red thread tag	**tail**	None
Silver mylar piping	**body**	Flat silver
None	**throat**	None
Peacock herl over white marabou	**wing**	White bucktail, green & black hackle
Nat. deer hair collar, trimmed	**cheeks**	Jungle cock

73 **NINE-THREE**
▶

◄
MARABOU STREAMER, YELLOW 72

2 to 12, 4X long	**hook**	4 to 12, 4X long
Black	**thread**	Black
Red wool, short	**tail**	Red goose
Embossed silver	**body**	Yellow floss, gold rib
Red hackle fibers	**throat**	Dark ginger
Peacock herl over yellow marabou	**wing**	Squirrel tail
None	**cheeks**	None

73 **PROFESSOR**
▶

STREAMERS

◀

RAINBOW TROUT 73
(*Thunder creek*)

6, 8 and 10, 6X long	**hook**	2 to 10, 4X long
Red	**thread**	Black, flat brown elk head
None	**tail**	Brown calf tail
Embossed silver, white bucktail belly	**body**	Cream fur, Red wool
Red thread collar	**throat**	None
Pink under green bucktail	**wing**	Red squirrel and furnace hackle
Yellow eye, black pupil	**cheeks**	None

73 SPUDDLER ▶

◀

RED AND WHITE BUCKTAIL 73

6 to 10, 4X long	**hook**	2 to 8, 6X long
Black	**thread**	Black
None	**tail**	Red wool
Silver, oval rib	**body**	Silver tinsel
None	**throat**	White hackle
Peacock over red & white bucktail	**wing**	Peacock over green & blue hackle, over white bucktail
None	**cheeks**	Jungle cock

73 SUPERVISOR ▶

◀

ROYAL COACHMAN 73

6 to 12, 4X long	**hook**	6 to 10, 4X long
Black	**thread**	Black
Golden pheasant tippet	**tail**	Red goose, gold tag
Peacock herl, red floss center	**body**	Yellow-orange fur, gold rib
Brown hackle	**throat**	Yellow hackle
White hackles (4)	**wing**	Brown bucktail
None	**cheeks**	None

74 WARDENS WORRY ▶

◀

SILVER DARTER 73

6 to 10, 4X long	**hook**	2 to 10, 3X long
Black	**thread**	Black
Silver pheasant wing	**tail**	Yellow fibers
White floss, silver rib	**body**	Black chenille, silver rib
Peacock sword	**throat**	Black hackle collar
Badger	**wing**	White bucktail
Jungle cock	**cheeks**	None

74 WESTERN BLACK GHOST ▶

◀

SILVER SHINER 73
(*Thunder creek*)

6, 8 and 10, 6X long	**hook**	4 to 12, 4X long
Red	**thread**	Black
None	**tail**	None
Embossed silver, white bucktail belly	**body**	Oval silver tinsel
Red thread collar	**throat**	Red hackle
Brown bucktail	**wing**	Peacock herl over brown & yellow marabou
Yellow eye, black pupil	**cheeks**	Jungle cock

74 YELLOW BREECHES STREAMER ▶

DRY FLIES

COLORADO KING 77

8 to 14	**hook**	8 to 18
Black	**thread**	Black
Two peccary fibers	**tail**	None
Yellow fur	**body**	Brown fur
Elk hair	**wing**	Poly yarn, brown
Grizzly palmer	**hackle**	None

77 **DIVING CADDIS FLY**

HEN SPINNER 77

6 to 22	**hook**	8 to 16
Black	**thread**	Black
Ginger fibers	**tail**	Brown fibers
Pale brown fur	**body**	Reversed hackle, fur
Hen hackle tips	**wing**	Blue dun hackle
None	**hackle**	None

77 **JORGENSEN HACKLE SPINNER**

SKATER 78

10 to 14, short	**hook**	10 to 18
Black	**thread**	Black
None	**tail**	Brown fibers
None	**body**	Reversed hackle, fur
None	**wing**	Mallard quill strips
Four large grizzly	**hackle**	None

78 **STILLBORN**

WET FLIES

MORSE'S ALDER FLY 76

8 to 16	**hook**	10 to 16
Black	**thread**	Black
None	**tail**	None
Black hair	**body**	Pheasant tail fibers, copper wire rib
None	**hackle**	Gray partridge
Black hair	**wing**	None

76 **PHEASANT TAIL**

NYMPHS

STARLING HERL 76

10 to 16	**hook**	10 to 16
Olive	**thread**	Black
None	**tail**	Blue dun fibers
Peacock herl	**body**	Yellow floss, pink fur
Starling covert	**hackle**	Blue dun hen
None	**wing**	None

77 **TUPS INDISPENSABLE**

EMERGER 74

12 to 18	**hook**	8 to 14
Black	**thread**	Black
Wood duck fibers	**tail**	Black hackle, trimmed
Medium brown fur	**body**	Grey-brown Seal-Ex
None	**thorax**	None
None	**legs**	Hackle, trimmed below
Grey hackle tips	**wings**	None. Wood duck antennae
None	**case**	Over body

74 **FLOATING CADDIS PUPA**

JORGENSEN LATEX STONE FLY 74

2 to 6, 3X long	**hook**	8 to 18
Black	**thread**	Black
Turkey wing fibers; antennae, same	**tail**	None
Brown Seal-Ex, quill rib	**body**	Latex strip, natural
Brown fur, rabbit	**thorax**	Dark-brown fur
Brown guard hairs	**legs**	Fur ficked out
None	**wing**	None
Latex; head, same	**case**	None

75 LATEX CADDIS PUPA

SOLOMON CADDIS PUPA 75

8 to 18	**hook**	8 to 14
Black	**thread**	Black
None	**tail**	Mini ostrich herl
Olive fur, dark thread rib	**body**	Tan Seal-Ex
Peacock herl	**thorax**	Tan Seal-Ex
Brown partridge; antennae, same	**legs**	Brown partridge
Mallard quill strips	**wing**	Mottled quill section
On sides	**case**	None

75 WIGGLE NYMPH

STREAMERS

JORGENSEN'S STREAKER 78

2 to 10, 3X long	**hook**	8 to 10, 4X long
Black or red	**thread**	Black
None	**tail**	Grizzly hackle fibers
None	**body**	Red floss; gold tag and rib
None	**throat**	Grizzly hackle collar
Deer body hair, shaped	**wing**	Woodchuck guard hair
Deer hair head, trimmed	**cheek**	None

79 LLAMA FLY

MATUKA 79

2 to 12, 4X long	**hook**	1/0 to 10, 3X long
Black	**thread**	Tan
None	**tail**	None
Red fur or yarn, gold rib	**body**	Tan fur; gold rib
Furnace hackle collar	**throat**	None
Two furnace hackles	**wing**	Two whole hackles
None	**cheek**	(Fins) Barred mallard breast
		Deer hair head, trimmed

79 MATUKA SCULPIN